PLOUGHSHARES

Spring 1996 · Vol. 22, No. 1

GUEST EDITOR
Marilyn Hacker

EDITOR
Don Lee

POETRY EDITOR
David Daniel

ASSISTANT EDITOR
Jodee Stanley

FOUNDING EDITOR
DeWitt Henry

FOUNDING PUBLISHER
Peter O'Malley

PLOUGHSHARES, a journal of new writing, is guest-edited serially by prominent writers who explore different and personal visions, aesthetics, and literary circles. PLOUGHSHARES is published in April, August, and December at Emerson College, 100 Beacon Street, Boston, MA 02116-1596. Telephone: (617) 824-8753. Web address: http://www.emerson.edu/ploughshares/.

EDITORIAL ASSISTANTS: Heidi Pitlor, Maryanne O'Hara, and Nathaniel Bellows. INTERN: Monique Hamzé. FICTION READERS: Billie Lydia Porter, Anne Kriel, Barbara Lewis, John Rubins, Karen Wise, Loretta Chen, Todd Cooper, Michael Rainho, Joseph Connolly, Holly LeCraw Howe, David Rowell, Emily Doherty, and Craig Salters. POETRY READERS: Lisa Sewell, Bethany Daniel, Mike Henry, Brijit Brown, Renee Rooks, Tom Laughlin, Lori Novick, Ellen Scharfenberg, and Jessica Purdy.

SUBSCRIPTIONS (ISSN 0048-4474): $19 for one year (3 issues), $36 for two years (6 issues); $22 a year for institutions. Add $5 a year for international.

UPCOMING: Fall 1996, a fiction issue edited by Richard Ford, will appear in August 1996. Winter 1996–97, a fiction and poetry issue edited by Robert Boswell & Ellen Bryant Voigt, will appear in December 1996. Spring 1997, a mixed issue edited by Yusef Komunyakaa, will appear in April 1997.

SUBMISSIONS: Please see page 217 for detailed submission policies.

Classroom-adoption, back-issue, and bulk orders may be placed directly through PLOUGHSHARES. Microfilms of back issues may be obtained from University Microfilms. PLOUGHSHARES is also available as CD-ROM and full-text products from EBSCO, H.W. Wilson, Information Access, and UMI. Indexed in M.L.A. Bibliography, American Humanities Index, Index of American Periodical Verse, Book Review Index. Self-index through Volume 6 available from the publisher; annual supplements appear in the fourth number of each subsequent volume. The views and opinions expressed in this journal are solely those of the authors. All rights for individual works revert to the authors upon publication.

PLOUGHSHARES receives additional support from the Lannan Foundation, the National Endowment for the Arts, and the Massachusetts Cultural Council. Marketing initiatives are funded by the Lila Wallace–Reader's Digest Literary Publishers Marketing Development Program, administered by the Council of Literary Magazines and Presses.

Distributed by Bernhard DeBoer (Nutley, NJ), Fine Print Distributors (Austin, TX), Ingram Periodicals (La Vergne, TN), International Periodical Distributors (Solana Beach, CA), and L-S Distributors (S. San Francisco, CA).

Printed in the United States of America on recycled paper by Edwards Brothers.

© 1996 by Emerson College

CONTENTS

Spring 1996

Introduction

It's been a great joy for me to work as an editor again, to have the privilege of sampling the range and richness of contemporary writing at its sources, and of compiling some of that writing in what's essentially a book, created as much by its internal juxtapositions as by individual pieces' indelible strengths. Prose and poetry share some of the same obsessions: we are at once corporeal and historical beings, existing in our physicality and our narratives, with the two often at odds. So Rosa Luxemburg and Antonio Gramsci discuss disability, AIDS is a silent communicant in a tea ceremony, Fanny Burney's mastectomy is lived through by a poet-survivor. The body of the text is itself closely examined: boundaries are permeated. Alfred Corn's poems and prose commentaries coalesce into a meditation on Bach, Kafka, faith, and history; Adrian C. Louis's anguished paragraphs rise and condense into the poetry of loss; Catherine Gammon examines the border of accountability between fiction and reportage.

Here at the end of the century there is AIDS, hunger, cancer, the shadows of Auschwitz and Hiroshima behind the vivid presence of those easiest to dismiss or dispossess: young black men, women with HIV, Spanish- or Arabic-speaking immigrants, people of ambiguous race or gender. When writers reflect on these presences, does it make for depressing reading? I'm elated, instead, at the bravado and dazzle these writers muster, staring down the void, at their virtuosity, their gourmandise for language—or languages—their eagerness to open the windows and doors of words on all their stories.

ELIZABETH ALEXANDER

Harlem Birthday Party

When my grandfather turned ninety we had a party
in a restaurant in Harlem called Copeland's.
Harlem restaurants are always dim to dark and this
was no exception. Daddy would have gone downtown
but Baba, as we called him, wanted to stay
in the neighborhood, and this place was "swanky."
We picked him up in his house on Hamilton Terrace.
His wife, "poor Minnette," had Alzheimer's disease
and thought Hordgie, who was not dead, was dead. She kept
cluck-clucking, "Poor Hordgie," and filling with tears.
They had organized a block watch on Hamilton
Terrace, which I was glad of; I worried always
about old people getting mugged; I was afraid
of getting old myself and knocked down in the street;
I was afraid it would happen to my grandfather.

My father moves fast always but in Harlem
something clicks into his walk which I love watching.
We argued about taking a car, about parking;
in the end some walked, some drove, and the restaurant
parked the car for us. They treated my grandfather
like a Pope or like Duke Ellington. We ate salad,
fried chicken, mashed potatoes, broccoli, chocolate
cake, and Gustavo, who was then my boyfriend, cut Minnette's
meat for her and that became one of the things I would cite
forever when people asked me, How did you know
you wanted to marry him? I remember looking
at all the people at the party I had never seen,
and thinking, My grandfather has a whole life
we know nothing about, like at his funeral,
two years later, when a dreadlocked man about my age
went on and on about coming to Harlem

from Jamaica, they all said, talk to Mister Alexander, and they talked, and my grandfather scolded,
advised, and today the young brother owns a patty stand
in Brooklyn. Who ever knew this young man, or all the rest?

The star appearance at Copeland's, besides my father, was
my grandfather's wife's cousin, Jane Tillman Irving,
who broadcast on WCBS all-news radio.
What is a Harlem birthday party without a star?
What is a black family without someone
who's related to someone else who is a little
bit famous, if only to other black people?

And then goodbye, and then goodbye, and back
to New Haven, Washington, and Philadelphia,
where I lived with Gustavo. We walked downtown
after the party to Macy's to get feather pillows
on sale, and then we took Amtrak home. I cannot think
about this party without thinking how glad I am
we had it, that he lived long and healthy, that two years
later he was gone. He was born in Jamaica,
West Indies, and he died in Harlem, New York.

Folding My Clothes

Tenderly she would take them down and fold
the arms in and fold again where my back
should go until she had made a small
tight square of my chest, a knot of socks
where my feet blossomed into toes,
a stack of denim from the waist down,
my panties strictly packed into the size
of handkerchiefs on which no trace
of tears showed: all of me under control.

But there was tenderness, the careful matching
of arm to arm, the smoothing of wrinkles,
every button buttoned on the checkered blouse
I disobeyed in. There was sweet order
in those scented drawers, party dresses
perfect as pictures in the back of the closet—
until I put them on, breathing life back
into those abstract shapes of who I was
which she found so much easier to love.

Two Years Too Late

*A Mexican migrant worker was kept sedated in an Oregon
mental hospital for two years because doctors couldn't
understand his Indian dialect. Hospital staffers
ruled Adolfo Gonzales was mentally ill because
"he couldn't speak to us to tell us he wasn't."*

These are the words you did not have
to tell them who you were,
Adolfo Gonzales.

Picking grapes in the cool blue fields,
you dreamt of a bigger life,
Adolfo Gonzales.

Of drinking the wine your work would make,
of wads as big as a bunch of grapes
in your own pocket.

You could taste the cream in your brewed café,
you could feel the rich soft leather
of your Cadillac.

You could almost touch the satin sheets
of the king-size bed you'd share
with the pretty blonde

you'd seen in a magazine in a store
where you bought tinned meat
with the cat label.

The next payday you went to town
to buy your girl and to wash your one
set of working clothes.

In the laundromat, you took them off
to wring out the earth you wanted
to leave behind you.

The next you knew, the police had come
with their hornet cars and their gunshot talk
to haul you off.

And you had no words they could understand
to say how you meant to dress as soon as
your clothes were done.

And you couldn't say how the blonde would want
a rich white man or at least a clean
brown one.

In a barred room like a caged bird,
you wailed songs from an old time
to the true gods

who would someday come and set you free
from the numbing pills
that tied your tongue.

You watched for them in that far sky
where the sun shone its gold coin
for the rich and poor.

Two years passed in a dazed blur.
Then the priest came with his nailed god,
and you spoke your name.

With a slurred tongue and a heavy heart,
you explained the dream you had dreamed before
they woke you up.

He isn't sick, so the priest said
to the white men who had locked you up.
He's an Indian man.

Adolfo Gonzales, I give you these words
that you did not have to tell them
who you were.

I am Adolfo Gonzales, set me free!
You are the ones who are sick for denying me
the good taste of the good life.

I am Adolfo Gonzales, set me free!

Breathing Lessons

Yet another Puerto Rican
Buddhist. He wants to breathe in
peace, while keeping his rice-
and-beans cooking skills, his accent,

his blue jeans from the Santana
years, his wine and rum collections
housed inside his head. Today's lesson:
fireflies know they're grasshoppers'

illusory stars. And that
Puerto Rico is only
a comma in Time's poem some
have called the Great Antilles.

The word "greater" is too much ego,
an egg which only revolution
can hatch. Fireflies in San Juan
around El Morro are gardens

with feet and wings. He breathes in. In.
It's the breathing out that is
difficult, for it's a loss. Loss
has, in the past, been his source of

knowledge. If he gives that up, then
loss will no longer be a gain, gains.
Meditation is like a game
of monopoly with his

Latino friends. It always ends
with a coup: the upturned board,
hotels thrown into the air,
useless *Get out of jail* cards,

a shower of dollars suddenly
worthless because of the players'
disbeliefs. He feels Puerto Rican
in New York, American

in San Juan, and Catholic
in Buddhist temples. He has blamed
karma for his bad Protestant
lovers. Joy is joy, even if

fleeting, or found when one is
being tortured. Buddha said that.
So did Genet. And Oliver Stone.
So does a fisherman friend who

sleeps with soldiers just to steal their
guns ("In case of an emergency
war!"). He isn't the reincarnation
of Che. He must find other

excuses to breathe below his waist.
His teacher warns him: *Forget yourself,
you are wind.* Does he want to let go
of memories, that Spanish entrée?

No more codfish, pork feet, chicken
breast stuffed with chickpeas and carrots,
steak with baby onions so it is
Venus wearing a pearl necklace.

He sits and waits not to be waiting.
He sits on toilets, sits on buses,
sits at his desk, sits at lunch
counters, sits in a lobby for

the latest physician who
will comfort him ("No, you're not dead").
He sits in the bathtub filled with tears for
an ancient water god long

evaporated into the air.
Baptists once told him to trust that
they would pull him out of the deep
end of the baptismal pool by

his Samson-like pubic hair.
He watches MTV's *The Grind* and
sees men and women reject their
childhood by running away with

their hips. His wet dreams drown him.
He wakes up gasping for air. But
Buddha teaches that most beaches
in Puerto Rico are illusions,

that the naked and the dead are
not obscene but opaque. He longs
for *home*. Longing is thinking so
he takes bigger breaths. In, in, in,

out. He is tired of being
the serpent of the Caribbean
in the tequila bottle. He
is no message floating in

the sea. He has nothing to say. He
is nothing. Nothing hurts his lungs. He
lunges into the Void. But he grows
afraid as he has been so many

countless times when his airplanes
began their descents into San Juan,
urban ghost that embraces
him until he too is breathless.

In the General

The anesthetist seems to bounce off the walls.
It is very late. As if underground
The trolley with my daughter crawls
With her ruined appendix. Wide and blue
The gowned anesthetist's speech is strange.
As he pats each wall, words flash from true.

His accent is thick as the paint's veined white
On the glimmering walls. He comes, I think,
From a country where thought ducked, down from sight.
"Have we a surgeon?" he asks the nurse
Who starts, then laughs. My daughter's lids flash.
In the building's bowels, her quiet grows worse.

"I have no knowledge of surgeons," insists
His voice. She sighs, tugs doors apart,
A number swings from my daughter's wrist.
Rooms shine with tubes. In self-defense
I glance away, then I translate.
He means, he has no confidence.

He knows, I know, there should be cries
So terrible the air would stop.
They struggle with the drip, which dries.
"She's out." As voices drown in water,
Night hides the unimagined day
I shout in anger at my daughter.

At the Playhouse

Nothing is like the theater. Backstage, with eighty children
I fight through wastes of plastic bags to youthful refugees.
They drop hairpins, lose their shirts or ask for biscuits,
Play guessing games or scrap till they are needed.
The oldest cries. The youngest, in a corner,
Intent as God, smears blue above her eyes.

They are not quiet: until that final moment
When curtains twitch, I thrust them at the light.
Some race back through the warren, past the drinkers,
Baskets of stores, with stories of disaster,
Who slipped: who fell.
                         Then I am left alone
Amongst the warm mounds of unwanted clothes.
I fold a shirt; hear singing stroke a window
Where the roof thrusts squarely black against night's blue sky,
This ugly building glimpsed for the first time.
Clear notes are cut off short where someone runs.

The audience sits fretfully. They see
The children's hurried play. They hear the guns.

Route 17

Just after I had landed my first job—
they needed busboys at the Mexican
chain restaurant that opened where Lake crossed
Route 17, an intersection known
in town for being dangerous—we met.
Among my new responsibilities
was polishing the silverware, he said
while pointing a dull butter knife at me.
He plunged it in a pitcher full of seltzer,
and for a moment it was diamond-jeweled
in carbonation, like some priceless dagger
belonging to a king.
                                        I wasn't fooled.
His muscle shirts and dancing skills combined
suggested his were pleasures of a sort
not more sophisticated, but *sublime*—
a word I memorized expressly for
the SATs. I planned to go away
to college—Massachusetts, maybe Maine,
which seemed as far from Jersey any place
could be. My parents didn't have the means
to pay the huge tuitions, so I had
to work. The friends I made, including Al,
agreed: what I needed to get ahead
was words.
                        He also managed a motel
for extra cash. He teased the waitresses;
the constant flirting reassured me. One
named Abby—poverty had made her wise,
at least to me, enamored of the green
tattoo inside her arm—suspected it.
Her ex and his best friend together formed

a band (they called themselves The Opiates)
which played at local clubs and senior proms
until they shocked her with the truth. "All queers
are obvious to me," she told me as
I kissed her tiny freckled breasts, unsure
of my performance.
                    Al was somewhere else
The night I got so drunk I could have done
whatever I imagined he might want
me to. They poured me Cuba Libres, rum
so sweet it made me want to stay, not quit
and go to college. Abby whispered in
my ear, her lips as thick as fingers: "Stay
with me." I wondered why he looked so thin.
I'd noticed how his clothes were ruffled by
the wind as he crossed 17 to get
his car; they seemed a size too big. Unclear
on who I was, I wanted him. "Forget
him, look at me," gnawed Abby on my ear.
I did.
            Just three months later, Al was dead.
It was the spring of 1983,
long before that shuttle with the astronauts
exploded. When I took the SATs
I thought of him, the night we saw that wreck
on 17. Six drunken teenagers
from town had crashed head-on into a truck.
Before the ambulance arrived, I heard
Al calling to them, darting underneath
the traffic light, the whole world stopped around
him. Trying crumpled doors, the oily heat
of radiator steam released, he found
their broken bodies first.
                            On 17,
he must have been infected; most rest stops
along the highway to New York were scenes
for cruising. Bodies pressed to bodies, cops
with flashlights peering into cars—today

it seems less glamorous to me. Back then,
the new disease that ravaged Al—("I'm gay,"
he finally confessed, above the din
of happy hour in the mirrored bar
as I was finishing my shift. "You need
a ride somewhere?" I hurried to my car...)—
seemed so momentous, meaningful as blood.
I wished I had been brave enough for him;
today, each word I learn seems guarded, grim.

Fairy Tale and Gloss

A wolf whose eyes glow red and jaws close quick
meets the voluptuous Miz Nude Bo-Peep
beside a shepherd with a crooked stick:
and, ever after, they enthrall lost sheep.

The wolf prowls round the shed. Straw, timber, brick—
he'll blow through walls, smash every windowpane.
But wait—he'll cut the sheep a deal. It's trick
or treat: just let the muttonheads ordain
a few for slaughter and he'll agree to rein
his wrath . . . those left stare past the bloody sill.
Too bad they never learned a martial skill
or paid attention in arithmetic.
(How many sacrificial lambs to fill
a wolf whose eyes glow red and jaws close quick?)

Bo-Peep always creates a stir. "She's cheap,"
one dam proclaims, "a common slut (excuse
my French!), but look at how these old tups leap
like yearlings: though they laze about, refuse
to trim the grass, stand drooping in a doze—
she bends to show that cleavage and—wham-bam—
your silly mate's transformed to horny ram."
Such vulgar dissipation makes her weep—
and what will happen when some little lamb
meets the voluptuous Miz Nude Bo-Peep?

The shepherd draws a square in dust: Magic!
A fence to keep the wolf far thence, contain
all helpless sheep, afraid, forlorn and sick.
He feeds them holy water and wolfsbane.
But should they stray, the crook can serve as cane

and send the fleeced flock tumbling down the hill
or stumbling panicked over stiles until
the round world has become his bailiwick
where lamb chops stretch out gladly on the grill
beside the shepherd with a crooked stick.

And everywhere they wander, there they reap:
bushels and bells, estates and revenues.
The wolf, well-sated, puts himself to sleep
counting his bags of wool, then dreams of queues
replete with shivering wethers, meaty ewes;
meanwhile, Bo-Peep (who now goes by "Madame")
rolls silken stockings up each shapely gam;
and the shepherd, owning lock and stock and keep,
has dubbed his crooked stick "The Great I Am"—
and, ever after, they enthrall lost sheep.

Musical Sacrifice

1.

Eisenach, birthplace (in 1685) of J. S. Bach. Close-by, on a high hill, Schloss Wartburg, the Thuringian landgraves' ancestral stronghold. Which also sheltered music, judging from Elisabeth's aria in Act II of *Tannhäuser*, a paean addressed to the castle's Great Hall as she waits for the Minnesänger to file in and join her. Music to fortify a fugitive Luther as well, who spent the winter of 1522 there, translating the Bible into dynamic German—and composing hymns. His chorale *Ein' Feste Burg* is most itself when set with strong supporting columns of vertical harmony, like a stone fortress built on some cloudflown crag overseeing the Kingdom. That high hill would also have cast its shadow over the boy Johann shortly after his father's death, which left him an orphan in the care of an exacting older brother.

(Chorale)
Passing through streets both small and broad
To Latin school, he hummed the theme
"A Mighty Fortress Is Our God,"
And stared up toward the snowbound castle.

Mother had died, and, after, Father.
Since Adam's fall we all must die,
Yet death stands warrant of our hope
To reach God's glorious court on high.

2.

Prague, baroque outpost of Austro-Hungary, birthplace (in 1883) of Franz Kafka. *Praha*, the "little mother with sharp claws," whose precincts were topped by a castle—Hapsburg decrees trickling down from it, with consequences for lives being led below in Czech, German, or Yiddish, a populace teeming across cobbled squares, men buttoned into the correct black suit with cravat, a bowler perched on their heads. From Malá Strana to Powder Tower to the Altneu *Shul*, magnetic fields fan out, the stone machine of category and rank in dependable operation.

(*Sprechstimme*)
Choose an unlikely figure, *Kaffeehausliterat*,
minor functionary, Jew, a glass ceiling
overhead, latest subject in the social laboratory,
which has him threading, like a white rat, baroque
labyrinths of alleys, streets, bridges and stairs
that might or might not lead to air and sunlight,

brilliant prospects over the town, intimacy with,
at decent distance, a Father in his stronghold.
But how to enter? *Das Schloss:* "castle" or "lock,"
His key, nothing more than lunch-hour daydreams...
Two fiancées in succession, intelligent,
sensitive; but not right, not right for him.

From the overlords, genteel racial disdain
but partly concealed. Parents, sisters, whose mere
health was a reproach to his own alienated body.
And writing: serious mistake, indeed, transgression, and yet
mandatory. Friends consoled themselves with music: him, though,
it overpowered, "like the sea," or a wall around his mind.

"I am chained to invisible literature with invisible chains."

3.
Having Journeyed on Foot to Lübeck to Hear Buxtehude, J.S.B.
Goes to the Sea and Watches a Horse and Rider on the Sands

(Toccata)
Crystalline cold, the rocking thunder
Adjunct to sun in galloping triples,
Sand underfoot, a sea to the right,
High waves of brine collecting to fall
In tumbling explosions, coldest of fires.

Will no wave rise without lifting the sun in replica?
O burn, O freeze, O burn!
Frozen starlike in the salt of a gallop,
A rocking thunder over the dunes, head bent
Forward next to the mane as a freezing stream
of diamond wind flames across horse and rider,
Sunburned by cold in a rocking sequence
Thundered back by the crash of a wave
Tipping over in a blue-and-gold gallop,
And must it stop playing its well-tuned welter
Of tangled blue manes, its foam-whitened gold?
O freeze, O burn, O freeze!
Rivered burning in the riptide gold,
Salty evangel declaiming triple thunder
That pounds an anvil of sand, the icy keyboard
Headlong hooves thunder over under the blue.
O burn, O freeze, O burn!
From triune Godhead comes the informing Spirit,
And gives us savor of eternity:
The soul borne upward on a faithful mount
By grace alone will scale high Heaven's ramparts.

4.
F.K. at Lugano (1911)

(Waltz)
Where lemon flowers constellate among dark leaves
and sweeten rising updrafts, water colors the view
for grand hotels, the lake staining deeper blue

at twilight to the flat clank of a church bell.
On the esplanade, yesteryear's white-haired string ensemble
dodders through something *echt* Viennese for guests

in boiled shirtfronts or mauve silk, sipping *aperitivi:*
the allure of lowered eyes, her enigmatic smile
borrowed from Mona Lisa, the late season's fatal

Madame X holding in thrall consumptive poet
or firebrand *metteur en scène,* who in her vibrancies
hears soaring Venusbergs or the final Liebestod.

"My dear Felice," F.K. would write a long year later,
"I feel as though I stood outside a locked door
behind which you live, and which never shall be opened."

Still later, after Franz Ferdinand had been shot
and the Great War unleashed, his daydream antidote
was sifting the potpourri of that lost era, when

malaise had infused the psyche only, a fragrant dust
in Europe's neurasthenic *Götterdämmerung,*
the switch thrown on ranks of Edison light bulbs,

whose moonglow set the stage for a drugged, experimental
waltz with dark specters, ultimate masked ball
of civilization on the eve of a blood cure.

5.
1722: Anna Magdalena's Little Clavier Book

(Allemande)
Among the lessons taught to all below
Are some that bear rehearsal more than once:
"We die, but when death comes we do not know."

My dear Maria died, almost as though
Early departure meant blest deliverance
From painful lessons taught to all below.

The thought of our children constrained to grow
Up orphans, paupers sunk in ignorance,
Could scarcely bear rehearsal more than once.

My early trials, how many years ago,
Were fruit of Father's undue confidence:
We die, but *when* death comes we do not know.

A second wife, then, fair, but not mere show,
Who'd let no child of Bach's turn out a dunce,
Teaching them lessons all must learn below.

Pride had demanded that I should forego
Love's gentle leadings. Gratefulest penance
Be mine to rehearse, then, and more than once.

Anna requested help with clavier, so
I put together a little book (a dance
Suite), and those ornaments she did not know

The fingering of, at last, began to flow.
Études, yet wrought and brought to utterance
By hard or tender lessons learned below—
Some of which bear rehearsal more than once:
We die, but when death comes we do not know.

6.

I discovered them both in 1963 and felt even then something resonant in the juxtaposition, two temperaments completely new and
yet somehow familiar. Long, late hours spent replaying the First
Brandenburg's Adagio, which conveyed better than any music
known to me before what might be called the *mysterium tremen-
dum,* an aura of sacred fear like a pearl-gray cloud between us and
unfathomable deity. Oboe, violin, and basses one after the other
state and restate the gradually descending theme against a shifting
ground of sustained string chords, bass line often the seventh of
dominant and secondary-dominant chords. The effect is of hard-
pressed determination, the soul testing its powers of understand-
ing when confronted with Creation from the first night until this,
the Dorian mode's rugged heft mustered to convey a sense of
ineluctable will accomplishing its ends in a world of mute suffering, the human particular left in the dark as to what upheavals

might mean or not mean while being subsumed under the Mystery.... And yet promised by abrupt modulations into major during the movement's final bars, to keep alive a sense of expectancy and replenishment. Which the last movement delivers.

As for reading Kafka, there will never again be a first encounter like that one, beginning, one cold February night, with *The Trial*, whose blinding glare didn't let me sleep until I'd raced, stumbling and falling, to the end. Transparent style and direct reporting of a character's dilemma activated fiction's deepest resource: identification, the I.D. in this case a set of papers that, far from constituting Josef K.'s protection under the law, in advance condemned him (like all outsiders—racial, cultural, sexual) to a final exclusion. "In the Penal Colony" came next, a courteous peep into Hell, describing some imaginary Devil's Island equipped with a machine designed to engrave sentences like HONOR THY SUPERIORS and BE JUST on the bodies of the condemned and self-condemned. And then *The Castle*, comedy at its most appalling, a pilgrimage, as much workaday as spiritual, through the frozen corridors of bureaucracy, in which red tape comes to resemble ribbons of blood flowing from the spot where administrative slapstick has struck a bit too hard on the petitioner's head, a stupid grin on his face as the Castle once more denies his request for an audience.

7.
1913: F.K. Publishes His First Book

(Scherzo in B-minor)
What, merely because your bumptious friend Brod
insisted you visit busy little Leipzig,
then flung you at *Meineherren* Rowohlt and Wolff;
and merely because those worthies professed to admire
some bleak-spirited trivia you call *Meditations,*

you bowed and let them serve the public *Kafka?*
Brilliant! Wasn't that you reading Heine last June
at your window, a bluebottle fly buzzing and bumbling

around your ears? Fly lit on page, then *bang!*
you snapped shut your book, which then fell open again:

Black goggle eyes and glassy winglets lay flat
around a speck of dark-red blood, in an instant
kaput and dry. Which triggered your brooding, "I am
that fly, who've done myself in." Ah, now the blunder
's been entombed in hard covers, are you content?

Write, if you must, but banish all thoughts of publishing!

8.

1723: Johannes-passion in Leipzig

(Recitative)
And it came to pass in those days
that the elders of the Council of Leipzig
summoned candidates for the post of Cantor
for St. Thomaskirche in the city,
among them, Johann Sebastian Bach.
The Council did not rule in his favor
but instead invited Telemann, who declined,
and then Graupner, who also declined.
"As the best could not be obtained,
we must take the second-rate."
So concluded the deliberations.

Yet the Council even so demanded
an example of sacred music wherewith
to judge the celebrated organ master;
thus did he compose a Passion
after the gospel that bore his name.
Not yet satisfied, the elders demanded
a letter of dismissal from the Prince,
his previous employer, and having at last
received it, installed the new Cantor
in June of that year of our Lord.

29

(Arioso)
And are they named St. Thomas Church to doubt
The man He is and works He has done, too?
Almighty God forgive the proud, who flout
Thy commandments, for they know not what they do.

And, Father, grant the strength to keep that head
Unbowed when henchmen come with jeers and flail:
A crown of thorns is well, so He be fed
On that high Love which cannot ever fail.

9. *1917: The Onset*

(Nocturne)
He had done as much as *will* can perform.
Had even moved into a fine apartment
in the Schönborn Palace, where you might live
decently with a new wife among vases of flowers—
as though you had left Prague behind, were less
in the grip of its musty stone fist.

Yet after her summer visit, he couldn't say.
Who stood, who watched, as her train withdrew, a phrase ringing
in his ears: *The alarm trumpets of nothingness?*
Utter oblivion. Early August doldrums sat
deathlike, burning leaves on all the lindens.... One day
he spat blood: his lungs' broken vessels had begun to speak.

To lie awake all night, headboard acreak in the heat,
unfinished drafts invisible in the darkness—
though he could, if need be, feel his way and find them.
A thunderstorm launched its bolts at the sleeping city,
quick volleys of unmeaning light, then giant drumrolls,
alarm trumpets of nothingness.... With dawn came rain,
gray light sifting through gently stirred curtain lace.

10.

Musikalisches Opfer, with no article, the noun always translated "Offering," though the German more often means "sacrifice," in the sense of sacred ritual. "Musical Sacrifice," then, one exacted by that musical monarch, Frederick II of Prussia, who had appointed Carl Philipp Emmanuel Bach his accompanist in 1740. The elder Bach was several times summoned to the Stadtschloss in Potsdam by his royal admirer, always refusing, until excuses courted insolence. So at last in May 1747, he came to his son's house in Potsdam, half-blind, weary, dusty from the journey. Word of his arrival reached Frederick at Sans Souci, who sent for him immediately, not even giving him time to change into court dress. The king canceled his customary Sunday evening musicale, and "der alte Bach" was ushered into the royal presence. Everyone has heard the story of Frederick's request: Will you sit at the clavier and improvise a fugue for us?

The composer asked the king to give him a theme and got a chromatic one in C-minor. Bach clasped his wrinkled hands, then took up the gauntlet to produce a three-part ricercare (the older term for a work with fugal texture), apparently delighting his audience. Then Frederick asked him to improvise a fugue with six voices, which Bach politely said he could not do: even mastery has its limits. On returning to Leipzig, however, Bach wrote out from memory the ricercare in three voices, devised another in six voices (responding to the king's challenge), and spun out as well ten more ingenious canons taking various approaches to the theme. One of these, subtitled "Per tonos," modulates up a whole step in pitch each time the canon repeats, rising higher and still higher as if scaling a mountain. Not often are technical stunts as expressive as this one, and yet it is less ingenious than other sections of the work, which take canonic texture to even higher levels of complexity. Considering the occasion and the labor voluntarily expended, it's clear why Bach might have given the name he did to the work, printed the following autumn with a dedication to Frederick and sent on to Potsdam like a bread-and-butter note.

Musical Sacrifice, like the more highly developed (though never completed) *Art of the Fugue,* is scored for no instruments in particular, a purely theoretical or pedagogical work reminding us that for Bach creation was happily married to instruction. He sought in these various realizations to produce not only a work of art but an exemplum as well of one or more technical features. No peak of formal difficulty was considered too steep to conquer—as long as sight and breath remained.

11. *A Sacrifice for Sans Souci*

(Canon)
Each year I take a step up the long stairs,
Remembrance flies to youth as to a glade:
The agile keyboard virtuoso tears
Through a fugue no middling fumbler could have played.

Remembrance flies to youth as to a glade
Where will delights in lively conversation
Through a fugue. No middling fumbler could have played
Like that, high ardor at one with calculation.

Where will delights in lively conversation
Take a young man? To marriage, for a start.
Like that high ardor at one with calculation
We have called "music," courtship won her heart.

Take a young man to marriage. For a start,
A child, then two, then more, like steps and stairs.
We have called music "courtship," one her heart
Quickened to hear, at times, quite unawares.

A child, then two, then more, like steps and stairs.
All talented! Whatever music they
Quickened to hear—at times, quite unawares—
I played and taught each one of them to play.

All talented! Whatever music they
May later master, this first shall not rust.
I played and taught each one of them to play
Exactly. Other things the best, I trust,

May later master. This first shall not rust.
Is not fine art, before all else, technique?
Exactly. Other things—the best, I trust—
The soul open to God will surely speak.

Fine art is not, beyond all else, technique.
The agile keyboard virtuoso tears
The soul open to God, who will surely speak
In each resounding step of the long stairs.

12.

Early in *The Castle*, K. attempts to get through to the palace offi-
cials by telephone, only to hear a sort of buzzing, "yet not a hum,
the echo of voices singing at an infinite distance—blended by
sheer impossibility into one high but resonant sound, which
vibrated on the ear as if it were trying to penetrate beyond mere
hearing." What happens when you associate those high voices
with the chorus of Bach's masterworks? Revived by Mendelssohn
early in the nineteenth century, the Passions according to
Matthew and John eventually became part of standard choral
repertory throughout Germany. Wagner knew these consum-
mately theatrical works; nothing easier than for him to consider
the anti-Jewish verses of the Passion text in the Gospel of John as
adjuncts (along with Luther's anti-Jewish writings) to his own
polemic in behalf of unalloyed Germanic genius. Bach's intentions notwithstanding, when audiences heard the call for cruci-
fixion attributed not to "the people," but to "the Jews," a
conscious or unconscious connection was established. Supreme
art fueling the onrush of historical evil.

F.K.'s escape from the Shoah was accidental: incurable tuberculosis killed him a decade before Hitler's Reich. TB was also the
metamorphosis that had been an excuse for breaking his second
engagement to Felice. With no wife to care for him, he had to rely
on the efforts of his youngest sister, Ottla, who took him to her
house in the country and tried to nurse him back to health. He
regained enough strength to travel to Berlin, where at last he met
Dora Diamant, the companion he had been seeking. A brief
period of happiness followed, unique in his experience. In April

of 1923 his friend Hugo Bergmann urged him to make literal the Passover promise of final return, a celebration "next year in Jerusalem." He had been studying Hebrew in an effort to recover the Judaic traditions that secular modernism had replaced. Emigration remained a possibility; but that next year, in terrible pain from tubercular throat lesions, he died, leaving *The Castle* incomplete.

Ottla had married a Czech Gentile, a legal status that, after Bohemia had been annexed by Germany, provided her with an immunity from deportation. She refused to profit by the loophole, however; fearing that her children would be implicated, she divorced her husband and registered as a Jew. She was first sent to Terezín and then volunteered to accompany a consignment of orphans being shipped to, she believed, Denmark, but in fact to Auschwitz. There, in October 1943, among searchlights, electric fences, and early snow, she died.

13. *Die Verwandlung*

(Symphonic poem)
We are nihilistic thoughts, *kafkas,* jackdaws,
crows in the mind of God,
who, as we do, has bad days—and thought of us
on one of His. Crows hoping to be translated
to Heaven as though unaware Heaven
to be itself requires the absence of crows.
Not to violate those precincts—do you follow, Ottla?—
we must prevent Heaven from thinking of us again.

One afternoon, high up on the Laurenziberg,
our Prague far down below, buildings built
all of smoke, block upon gray block of smoke,
I watched a flock of crows
mount up into the sky in a long line and thought,
Those wings are bookbindings, and our books, the steps
of a staircase that breaks off in the sky—
No, rather, a book is a key to the hidden rooms

within the fortress of one's own self,
a black key having the shape of a crow.

I ought to be able to invent words
capable of blowing the odor of corpses in a direction
other than straight into mine and the reader's face.
It was wrong, Ottla, to have allowed those thoughts
to enter your mind—and to bring my illness
to your house, where without the ghost of a complaint
you tried to restore an ailing elder brother
to health again, whether or not he believed you could.
If I could have written myself well again for you!

Once, after you had fed us a small supper,
we sat by the hearth at a low fire,
an orange glow wavering among communicating coals.
A sheaf of gold chrysanthemums sat on top of the piano.
The vase replaced one my elbow had knocked over,
inadvertently, a few days before.
I watched you shovel ashes into a bin, and a daydream,
no, some cinematic phantasm overtook me.
A spark from the coals leapt to my mouth and burned
my lips—but burned away as well the pain of burning.
I saw ashes falling from a great height through space,
falling, falling, as though they might never
get to the bottom of things.
And was tempted to look for their source,
some altar or furnace high up that had produced them;
say, vast numbers of crows heaped up together and burned.
What made me turn away from those images?
Who knows, but they were replaced in thought by a music—
frightening, yet one that I, who always avoided music,
didn't choose not to hear. The figure running across
the keyboard was myself, my footfalls
sounding the notes; and others were running,
fleeing from the catastrophe, each foot
landing on a key as, unawares, we all cooperated.
Was it a fugue of death, a human counterpoint

made by fugitives? Composing not the music
we'd have otherwise produced, but what our flight
from death wrung out of us collectively.

A great hand like the shadow of a bird
approached and began removing, in mid-flight,
each running figure,
so that voices of the fugue, one by one, dropped out.
Until, at length, no more than two of us remained,
who then stopped running. Oh, but
it was you, Ottla, you were the other,
standing there on a white key, and I, on a black one.
Having so much to say meant we could say nothing,
and nothing inhabited the space between us,
a nothing that bloomed full and golden.
Then I felt myself being taken up; yet didn't tear
my gaze from yours until its silent music
had been translated into darkness,
all my nothing consenting to be absent from the world.
The Holy of Holies opened and nothing was in it.
You were free, Ottla, your name no longer "Kafka,"
and thus were allowed to live. This is why I fell silent—
do you recall?—that dark afternoon by the fire.

14. *1750: J.S.B. Dictates His Last Work from the Deathbed*

(Chorale Prelude)
When we in greatest need do call
Upon His name, may Jesu send
His strong assistance lest we fall,
And help us make a holy end.

When I in sorest need, in blindness, must
Prepare to bid farewell, my labors done,
The hand that rests upon my brow, I trust
As Love that nothing shall divide me from.

This life has been a prelude and a vale
Where all things teach Thy children Who Thou art.
So may the faithful not forget to hail
Thy cross and glory, Lord, when they depart.

Before Thy throne I shall have trod,
To hear the judgment held in store,
The plea I offer nothing more
Than that Thou diedst for me, O God.

The grace that was and is sufficient guides
Even the lost sheep safely to the fold.
Sing, blessèd choirs of angels as of old:
"Nor Sin nor Death prevails where Love abides!"

Amen, Alleluia, Alleluia, Amen, Amen.

My Questions to Obachan, Her Answers

In barracks, Grandma, did dust chafe your lips?
The men played poker, the women played bridge.

And guards, rifles, the chain of black sleek boots?
The girls cut out dolls, ripped paper in skirts.

Or towers, gleaming, plugged with silver barrels?
The copperheads slid through tundra and thistles.

My mother, born in camp, draining your milk?
Their hides snagged in the fence, wires lined with snake.

And Grandpa, prairies east, did he send mail?
Boys slit the throats, black venom dripped from scales.

Your son, a soldier, gutting Nazis in France?
They batted rocks, swatted coal through the fence.

Why give me sticks and skirts, these dolls and fangs?
Dusk broke like a flag, the red sun of Japan.

Atomic blasts across seas, trains toward home?
I stared in mirrors, plucked hair from my comb.

Your church, Japantown, gold arch of the Bay?
I read my husband's words: "Some nights, I pray."

And Grandma, now you've left the camps, the war?
I snapped off the lamp, the guards closed my door.

A Conversation with My Mother, Renko, About the Journey to and from "Manzanar War Relocation Center" in a Dream

A lotus is a lotus.
A train is a train.

No, this train is a lotus, this lotus is a train.

The petals are white swords.
The engine a head of steam.

No, petals are spumes of ash blooming from this train.

The bud opens to water.
The pistons drive with flame.

No, this train drives down the zone of the stem, a cold black
  tunnel.

A lotus is a flower.

No, this lotus is your cold body wrapped in cotton.
This bud is your lips muzzling milk
from your mother in the smoky compartment.

A boxcar is a train.

No, your mother is this train and her eyes are blue cones
slicing mist in radiant columns. The boxcars slide
down the stem like drops of dark water.

You insist I wanted to be this lotus,
I wanted to board this train?

No, the stem is not a lotus in mud
but you buried knee-deep in a camp full of shit.
Your barrack is a box of panes and iron,
your camp a coal splitting with dust and plains.

The lotus may have been lost in the desert.
The desert may have been found in the train.

No, the train is a string of boxcars.
Each boxcar a chunk of dust I pluck from your stem.
Your stem is a mile of sharp, thistled wire.

I see a bulb sliding in you, my father.
Black steel ripping mist from tunnels. Your mother.
Steam and heat cleanse the walls. This is your lover.
A boy dripping with water is me, the son.

Mother, maybe barbed wire is milk, nipples floods
of lights, the granite peak a triangle of hair,

...this soot is a flower,
your breath a wisp of burnt coal,
your hair silver rail, your spine a track...

...veins are barracks, your knuckles
tarpaper, this steel tower your throat,
this lotus your fist, your breath sleek wire...

...your breast is my mouth, my tongue milk
your fingers white swords,
this stem your breath, it grew from flesh and dirt...

A lotus might not be a lotus.
A train might not be a train.

TORY DENT

Everybody Loves a Winner

"Freedom's just another word for nothing left to lose."
—Janis Joplin

But when you lose it's only you and the hard wood maple floor
beneath you, your shoulders pinned down, wet shirt on a
  clothesline
by the knees of a god leather-clad in medieval thigh-highs.
He forces you to repeat or he'll show you his fist again
a hot pool has already boiled up in your throat—
your head to the side you watch red rivet on the polyurethane
  finish
the splattering on his gray T-shirt when you give him what he
  wants
"Our Father who art in heaven" and you've got to get it right
no tone of sacrilege, nothing but the pure submission
that the purgatorial twilight outside has brought about
this epic plot eschatological in proportion
where you are the dot in a pointillist painting,
the undetectable one, the point of vanishing
the streaks of amethyst and taupe underscore the sky's
  authenticity
It's hard to believe that you ever thought it beautiful
hasn't reality always been by virtue of the realistic aspect always
  horrible
like the real rope that ties your ankles and wrists together,
prepared like the modern-day equivalent of a virgin for slaughter
a stiff strapped to a cake of cement en route to the East River
and you can't feel anything from your pelvis on down
you look forward to nothing in totality now that your options
  have run out.

Everybody loves a winner, but when you lose it's just you and the
  partial view

out the hospital window, just you in front of the doctor when he
    tells you
you're too hopeful, just you and less than that for you're
    shrinking, melting,
you are that which is diminishing like a snowbank in February
like the wicked witch of the west destroyed by drinking water
just you and the self-conscious stratum of your prayers
wherein its tapestry you are less than water and the verdigris
    thread
that depicts the facial details of those who will go on without you
the winners with torsos built with such genetic supremacy
they appear manufactured, checked once for efficiency like an
    Icelandic horse
then set free like wild ponies on the Côte d'Azur.
Everybody loves a winner but when you lose it's you who's
    watching the ponies
your individuality instantly annihilated in the category of
    spectatorship,
drowning in the oceanic still life that backdrops their wildness
the waves pitched in churlish peaks like cake frosting or moussed
    hair
the trends of teal and navy like the subway map of your body's
    meridians
for all of life has becomes paradigmatic of your interiority in its
    finitude
the seminary belfry the diagrammatic sonata for the intricacy of
    your despair
this particular December evening when you actually *feel* the
    winners gather
together in the chapel and an hour later in the mess hall
and mutter their gratitude for genetic technology and the more
    secure
sense of community it's produced like electric fencing.
When you lose it's just you watching the electric fence, like a cow
with your flat brow and slight furrowed brown eyes that steady
    themselves
as only a sign from which no signification can be wrought

not by theologian, semiotician, vegetarian, or third-generation
    farmer.
Oblivious to the slaughter number tattoo on their ears as their
    nostrils flare in the just-above-freezing air, they watch the
    humans
scurry back to the hutch where a singular trail of chimney smoke
    promotes
a sense of gradation and process amidst a darkness that descends
in one monolithic and monochromatic movement like the
    guillotine.

Everybody loves a winner, but when you lose it's just you and
    your bedroom
as an antechamber, the snuffbox of the bed itself where like ash
    inside
a mastaba you have already returned to white powder. I have
    returned already
to Mecca, to Minnesota, to my future fast-forwarded in the
    multiminute
of my being forced to focus on my mortality at such a young age
like the repeated refrain of a psychopathic rapist to keep him
    from raping me
I'll stare into the pupil the dilating finality, a kind of
    metaphysical dual
where the stakes pierce themselves like harpoons into what's
    purely physical
and win by deferral, by a Buddhist acknowledgment of the
    world's inequality
and return already, ahead of schedule, to fray from fabric, to tree
    from text
I'll watch the wild ponies from an aisle seat in business class
that flies solo sans 747 chassis, having already experienced the
    crash.
I'll win by losing, by looking up at the winning sky from a six-
    sided box
for nothing is lonelier than a grave, mass or single, shallow or
    deep

determined or ubiquitous like the eccentric wishes for the at-last
unfettered ashes to be sprinkled like fairy dust over a favorite
  mountain range.
I'll give birth to myself by virtue of my degradation,
lick the self-inflicted wounds of my masochism,
carry a pea on my nose in the effort to perfect my posture
and take it on the chin as the British would say.
I'll lose by winning, take the sky like a phallus into my mouth
and subsume what's impossible to subsume by the degree of my
  subordination.
Everybody loves a winner, loves the credit card, gold or green
when it's taken out to pay for dinner. Everybody loves the New
  Jersey upstart,
the unmanicured beauty, the wizened scholar who's revered in
  part
for his hideous appearance. And everybody loves Magic Johnson
even more than ever now that he's HIV-positive
but they don't love my dead friends, and they don't love me
  neither
they don't love a loser unless you were good first at athletics.
Everybody loves a winner. I love them true myself.
it's just that I recognize the loser from my own lonesome state,
one tree to another, from across a forest, the matte green tennis
  lawn
at Wimbledon, like "Some Enchanted Evening," as having won at
  something else.

Voice as Gym-Body

In order for a rapprochement with the physical body
Only necromancy could be behind it.
Racked on a stretcher the I.V. tubes string me up
like a cello without a player

Only necromancy could be behind it.
These days of horse-drawn betrayal.
Like a cello without a player
I'm caught, a crown of thorns, in a winter orchard.

These days of horse-drawn betrayal.
Impromptu night: tar ridge.
I'm caught, a crown of thorns, in a winter orchard,
a keyboard silent as the keyboard to deaf Beethoven.

Impromptu night: tar ridge.
I insert the child's hand literally into my chest,
a keyboard silent as the keyboard to deaf Beethoven.
As if a surgeon's, I warm it.

I insert the child's hand literally into my chest.
Fingers twitch like an impulse, final and emotive
As if a surgeon's, I warm it
with my voice (overbuilt to compensate for no child).

Fingers twitch like an impulse, final and emotive.
The way one man survived was by altarpiece commissions.
With my voice (overbuilt to compensate for no child)
like an altarpiece, I try continually to build.

The way one man survived was by altarpiece commissions.
Racked on a stretcher the I.V. tubes string me up
like an altarpiece I try continually to build
in order for a rapprochement with the physical body.

Blacks in the U.

There is a new black woman in the English department. Several people told me about her, that she is extremely nice, and that she looks white—like me. The way they described her, I didn't know what I'd see, though I think I thought to myself, *Another "nice" light-skinned girl who knows how to make people like her.* I thought, *Well, I guess either I've done a great job and they've decided they can get along with light-skinned black women, or well, here is the light-skinned black woman who is* still *nice, the one coming to take my place.*

I was sitting in a colleague's office and a nice-looking young woman stuck her head in the door. My colleague introduced us, *This is the new person on staff.* She was so happy to meet me, I realized this must be the young woman I had heard so much about—the brilliant, sweet, pleasant, lovely, new black woman who looks white. I suddenly had that feeling that I was looking at her through something—that I had backed up fifty yards to stare at her through a pinhole. Either she was showing something or I was seeing something so much in contrast to what I wanted to see that I didn't want to see it.

I was (1) seeing if she really *did* look white, (2) seeing if she looked as white as *me*, (3) saying, *She's young, beautiful, charming, I'm on the way out,* (4) and I was in love with her, too—she is graceful, (5) saying, *She's nice to me now, but I will soon let her down,* (6) saying, *She's trying to get something from me, she'll use me, hurt me,* (7) thinking—*Oh my God, they've brought in another one. Then, I really* am *here, not because of me, but because that's the only skin they can tolerate.* And I thought how sad it is that we *are* here, either because we *are* the only people they can find, or because they want us to be. I felt despairing and helpless.

Having lunch with her, all the feelings persisted, the fears and attractions. And I realized that something rare had happened when I saw her.

Often, when I see a black person, after having been in an all-white environment like this one for a long time, I experience a kind of shock, as if I've forgotten I'm black, and seeing that person makes me remember. It often comes upon me with a feeling of dread and revulsion, as if I'm looking in a mirror I don't want to see, and I have great shame about these feelings. But when I realized *she* is black, I felt another kind of distancing—the shock of recognizing what *I* look like. I said to myself, *So this is what it is to look white to others.* I felt a kind of disbelief, a lack of trust, as if something about her was deliberately deceitful and I had to watch out. And then I felt great fear for myself, for how I must be judged.

I have written about that sudden feeling of distance and alienation when I see a dark person that has so disturbed me. I had thought if I acknowledged it, told the truth, if I admitted how racism has been internalized, then that awful feeling would go away. I had thought that that reaction was connected to seeing someone dark, a dark man, for that is the one I thought we had been taught mostly to hate and fear. But now I see that that moment of separation and fear can be attached to anyone, that sometimes it is a honey-colored woman or even a child, that just as there is an internalized picture of a hated and feared dark person, there is also a picture of hated and feared light woman, and she looks like *me*. Perhaps if you are black, no matter what color you are, there is something wrong, there is no safe color. And perhaps there are even deeper structures than racism that keep us from touching the most fearful aspects of our own natures.

· · ·

She did seem well-mannered, considerate, kind, and quick to help. When a waiter broke a glass, she bent down immediately to help him pick up the broken pieces. Instead of thinking, *How kind she is,* I thought, *She's just trying to impress me.* Or, *Why didn't I think to do that?*

Later, we exchanged mother stories and talked about the difficulty of separating, especially of establishing ourselves as our own women, our sexual lives. She is trying to live on her own, to be separate from her mother, and it is very hard, since for years her mother was her best friend. I could tell she feels a great deal of sadness and fear about these changes. I told her that the first thing my mother had said to me when I was born was, *I will never be alone again.* And how, when I went home this last time and tried to be that "Toi" who entertained my mother, the sweet, funny, good girl, telling funny stories and gossiping, I couldn't do it. (My poor mother, who thought my love would replace the love of the mother who had died when she was eighteen; and me, the poor daughter of a woman who took every hint of separation as a betrayal.) I knew eventually the old partings would come, and that sudden and terrifying feeling of disappointment and separation would come over me. I told her that what I grieved for most was not the relationship with my mother, but the part of me that couldn't go back and be that thing that had tried so hard to please her, to stay connected, the part that now felt so distant and guarded, so isolated and strange. *Who am I if I am not the one I used to be?*

. . .

It's funny. Seeing her begins with race and color and ends with us talking about our mothers, about separating and being a grown-up, and I wondered if that great grief of separation is connected to all these other moments of space between us—even the spaces of race and color.

Sometimes I think that eventually every identity breaks down to some self that has to learn to live between loneliness and connection, stuck in some primal way in a spot one cannot retreat from. I don't mean that being black can ever be a lost identity in this racist world, or that it should be. I don't mean anything like those people who say, I don't see color. But that in some way even our connections to the ones most like us become unsolid, unreal, and, though there is a necessity for trust and commitment, in another way we are nothing more than some kind of spirit-movement walking through the world clothed in a certain story of its life.

Perhaps this revulsion for the other is really a revulsion for my own self, my own fears of being "other," separate and alone. Perhaps accepting this distance, even from the ones most like me, the ones I love and would like to be closest to, is really the way I will finally see us as we truly are, all of us "other," frighteningly distant from each other, and yet needing and loving each other.

. . .

I remember a game I used to play in childhood, it was one of my favorite games and I played it for years. I would put myself in my grandmother's pantry behind the gate where they locked the dog, and I'd play "elevator," closing the gate, going up, opening. It may have been enacting a fear, for my grandmother was terrified of elevators and wouldn't go into a store or building if that was the only way she could go up, and it has been a fear of mine, too. For years I wouldn't get on a plane, and I was terrified to be on a bridge that was crowded and I couldn't get off, to be somewhere, anywhere, where I couldn't have access to something, somebody who loved me, who would save me from feeling alone. The anxiety was unbearable. I couldn't stand to be cut off and left to my own feelings of distance and terror.

. . .

I hear the dogs whining next door. Maybe they are locked up. I think of but can't imagine that feeling of being shut away again and again, weeping and begging, humiliated and in incredible pain, and going through it every day, every day forgetting what it felt like and coming out and loving those same people again, as if every day the part that loves is regenerated and then torn off again, like people coming back to live the same life over and over, and you can see it from a distance and know that every day they are going to have to live that same pain.

Or perhaps being alone you make up your mind to like it, to be in there thinking or talking to yourself or looking out the window or making up a game or a poem, and suddenly you're glad you're alone, you don't want them to come anywhere near you, and you feel like only if you're alone can you have your own life, write your own poetry, think, be, and hating the fact that maybe they might want you, call you, expect you to pay attention.

And then starting to like being with them, starting to trust that they can listen to you, that you can orchestrate the space between you so that you don't feel destroyed, taken advantage of. You can do it the other way, you can have your own separate and isolated life, but still, for a moment, here, it almost feels as if someone understands you and you understand that person, and you begin to think, Well, why not want everything different, why not begin a new way? and you think, Well, now maybe forever.

. . .

Race isn't a metaphor. Color isn't a metaphor. It doesn't feel like a metaphor. It hurts as if it's my skin. I feel sick. I hate myself. I make you hate me. I separate. I come back. Forgive me. This is the best I can do.

. . .

What I discovered when I saw the other white-looking woman in my colleague's office was that I loved her, was that going down into any "other"—as I might now be able to go down into my own self's "otherness," I find everything intact I was made to put out of me. Not just the dark person, but the light one, too, and the colors between, and the too fat and the too skinny and the frightening, dangerous father, and the weak, depressed one, and the huge white God with his head like a smokestack, and the beaten dog, and the mother scrubbing the tub out with a rag, and the grandmother in her quilted death, and the other mother with her long black hair braided on top of her head like a crown, and the poor boy standing over me with a knife who stank of pee and nearly took my life, and my own beautiful son, and my gold grandson, and the white and black of what we have all been called, and, even deeper, that blank moment of nothingness and separation that I fear more than my own death.

. . .

Never show your fear, my father always said when we'd see a big dog, *they can smell it.* But it is fear that I have acknowledged and taken in.

from *Brutal Imagination*

*The speaker is the young black man Susan Smith
claimed kidnapped her children.*

How I Got Born

Though it's common belief
That Susan Smith willed me alive
At the moment
Her babies sank into the lake

When called, I come.
My job is to get things done.
I am piecemeal.
I make my living by taking things.

So now a mother needs me clothed
In hand-me-downs
And a knit cap.

Whatever.
We arrive, bereaved
On a stranger's step.
Baby, they weep,
Poor child.

My Heart

Susan Smith has invented me because
Nobody else in town will do what
She needs me to do.
I mean: jump in an idling car
And drive off with two sad and
Frightened kids in the back.
Like a bad lover, she had given me a poisoned heart.
It pounds both our ribs, black, angry, nothing
    but business.
Since her fear is my blood
And her need part mythical,
Everything she says about me is true.

Who Am I?

Who are you, mister?
One of the boys asks
From the eternal back seat,
And here is the one good thing:
If I am alive, then so, briefly are they,
Two boys returned, three and one,
Quiet and scared, bunched together
Breathing like small beasts.
They can't place me, yet there's
Something familiar.
Though my skin and sex are different, maybe
It's the way I drive
Or occasionally glance back
With concern,
Maybe it's the mixed blessing
Someone, perhaps circumstance,
Has given us,
The secret thrill of hiding
Childish, in plain sight,
Seen, but not seen,
As if suddenly given the power
To move through walls,
To know every secret without permission.
We roll sleepless through the dark streets, but inside
The cab is lit with brutal imagination.

Sightings

A few nights ago
A man swears he saw me pump gas
With the children
At a convenience store
Like a punchline you get the next day,
Or a kiss in a dream that returns while
You're in the middle of doing
Something else.

I left money in his hand.

Mr. ____ who lives in ____
South Carolina,
Of average height
And a certain weight
Who may or may not
Believe in any of the
Basic recognized religions,
Saw me move like an angel
In my dusky skin
And knit hat.

Perhaps I looked him in the eye.

Ms. ____ saw a glint of us
On which highway?
On the street that's close
To what landmark?

She now recalls
The two children in the back
Appeared to be behaving.

Mr. ____ now knows he heard
The tires of the car
Everyone is looking for
Crush the gravel
As we pulled up,
In the wee, wee hours
At the motel where
He works the night desk.

I signed or didn't sign the register.
I took or didn't take the key from his hands.
He looked or forgot to look
As I pulled off to park in front
Of one of the rooms at the back.

Did I say I was traveling with kids?
Who slept that night
In the untouched beds?

Atomic Bride

for Andre Foxxe

A good show
Starts in the
Dressing room

And works its way
To the stage.
Close the door,

Andre's cross-
Dressing, what
A drag. All

The world loves
A bride, something
About those gowns.

A good wedding
Starts in the
Department store

And works its way
Into the photo album.
Close the door,

Andre's tying
The knot, what
A drag. Isn't he

Lovely? All
The world loves
A bachelor, some-

Thing about glamour
& Glitz, white
Shirts, lawsuits.

A good dog
Starts in the yard
And works

Its way into
Da house.
Close your eyes,

Andre's wide open.
One freak of the week
Per night, what

A drag. All
The world loves
A nuclear family,

Something about
A suburban home,
Chaos in order.

A good bride
Starts in the
Laboratory

And works
His way
To the church.

Close the door,
Andre's thinking
Things over. All

The world loves
A divorce, something
About broken vows.

A good war starts
In the courtroom
And works its way

To the album cover.
Close the door,
Andre's swearing in. All

The world loves
A star witness, something
about cross-examination.

A good drug starts
In Washington
And works its way

To the dance floor.
Close the door,
Andre's strung out,

What a drag.
Isn't he lovely? All
The world loves

Rhythm guitar, some-
Thing about
Those warm chords.

A good skeleton
Starts in the closet
And works its way

To the top of the charts.
Start the organ.
Andre's on his way

Down the aisle,
Alone, what an encore. All
The world loves

An explosive ending.
Go ahead, Andre,
Toss the bouquet.

Offerings to an Ulcerated God

Chelsea, Massachusetts

"Mrs. López refuses to pay rent,
and we want her out,"
the landlord's lawyer said,
tugging at his law school ring.
The judge called for an interpreter,
but all the interpreters were gone,
trafficking in Spanish
at the criminal session
on the second floor.

A volunteer stood up in the gallery.
Mrs. López showed the interpreter
a poker hand of snapshots,
the rat curled in a glue trap
next to the refrigerator,
the water frozen in the toilet,
a door without a doorknob.
(No rent for this. I know the law
and I want to speak,
she whispered to the interpreter.)

"Tell her she has to pay
and she has ten days to get out,"
the judge commanded, rose
so the rest of the courtroom rose,
and left the bench.
Suddenly, the courtroom clattered
with the end of business:
the clerk of the court
gathered her files
and the bailiff went to lunch.

Mrs. López stood before the bench,
still holding up her fan of snapshots
like an offering this ulcerated god
refused to taste,
while the interpreter
felt the burning
bubble in his throat
as he slowly turned to face her.

On Worms, and Being Lucky

Two kinds of sand. One heavy, gritty,
That falters moodily under your toes, like custard;
The other, shiny weedy ribs, and further,

Out of sight, the standstill sea. You tramp along
In sunbonnet and spade, summer's regalia.
You choose a gray snake's nest, slice into it,

And yes, there *are* lugworms, and you carve them out,
And he hoicks you up, your dad, to the space round his head.
You've got the knack, my princess, he says. *You're lucky.*

Then there's your turn for betting. Bored by favorites,
You always picked the unfancied outsider.
The field foundered at Becher's. Or something.

Anyway, yours won, against the odds
(*Lucky, my princess!*) since you knew it would,
And knew it into winning. (*Sweetheart. Lucky.*)

After the operation, you were sent for.
(He was propped up in bed, reeking of ether,
Possibly dying.) You held the big limp hands,

And lugged him back to life, like a cow from a bog.
He clung to your luck, and kept it
For two more years. You gave him something,
Not knowing what it was. (*The knack,* he wheezes.)

Or love, maybe. Two kinds of luck.
My luck, dear Father, flashy and absurd,
A matter of long odds and stop-press news;

Yours was the gift that sees life gold side up,
So that a knack of finding worms becomes
A serious blessing.

Née

She had strong views on Mrs. Humphry Ward,
The Brontës, poor souls, women called George,
Novelists known as A Lady.

                         There was always
An edginess. Whenever we went too far,
Children or parent, she'd flare *Oh you Fanthorpes!*
As if at some foreign breed.

She lost some magic when she married us.
Not race or class, but a sense of being her.
Red hair was part of it, and the surname
That gave her the convent's nickname, *Reddy.*

Marriage turned her *Ginger;* and unsettled her.
We knew the men who might have been our father,
Doctor, diplomat, soldier. We understood
They'd have had better, smarter children.

The way she said *My* family left us standing.
Racier than anything we knew, her father,
The seventh son, who wouldn't marry the heiress,
Walked from Devon to London, his flute in his pocket;

Her handsome mother, lover of dogs, not children,
Descendant of the gentle Tudor scholar,
Who never used a fullstop in her life.

She did everything well. Had a head for figures,
Understood the Married Women's Property Act.
Created faultless parcels, F's and P's flamboyant,
Converted the exile of marriage into art.

Vaguely we knew we'd missed something by happening.
We were the children of Mrs. Humphry Ward.
Marriage is burial, she used to say.

I could have written novels, or played the French horn.

JULIE FAY

Hannah

from *In the Houses of the Good People*

When I was a girl I had a place in the stable I'd go to be alone. I cleaned it of all the spider webs and laid down a layer of fresh straw. When Mother began her travail with Elizabeth, I went there to get away from the sound of her pain. I was seven. After a while, I went back into the house. The midwife, Mary Neff, had arrived, wearing her cape and carrying a large satchel. Mother stood near the window, large as a nightmare in her linen shift, drinking groaning ale from a small tankard. Her long braid hung down to her waist. The dinner board was spread with the "groaning" cakes we'd spent weeks preparing, with quince and pippin and damson marmalades. There was a goat cheese. Mother thudded the mug and grabbed the mantle. She panted like a dog in July, her knees slightly bent. She had little bits of sweat on her brow. She concentrated hard, looked down at her feet. From the bottle in her hand, Goody Whittier poured a spoonful of betony tonic, that dark, thick liquid that is so vile going down but helps the pain substantially. Mother was in much pain and Mary sent me for some sheep's wool from the barn. When I returned, Mother was on the bed, propped against a sack of rags. Mary pulled her shift up and pressed the wool to the side of Mother's swollen belly, saying it would help until the betony did its job. I was disgusted by the ample shock of dark hair in Mother's private area. Would I get hair there—bushy and dark as that? I stayed quiet and listened to the women talk.

"You take a lock of virgin's hair on any part of her head, and half the age of the woman in travail," said Mary Neff. "Then you cut it very small to fine powder. Then two ants' eggs you've dried in an oven after your bread is drawn or otherwise made dry and make them, too, into a powder with the hair," she continued. "Give this with a quarter pint of red cow's milk or for want of it give it in strong ale wart. That will serve for a sharp and difficult travail as well as sheep's fur," said Mary. "But I used the last of it last night with Goody Swan's delivery."

When it was just about time, Mary ran her hand over the large lump of butter I had fetched from the pantry. She scooped a good bit of it in her hand, and rubbed it amply between Mother's legs. I could see Mother's opening now, as large as my fist. How long would it be before the little hole my finger fit perfectly into got to be that large? It frightened me. When Mother screamed I felt hot and dizzy and was afraid I would fall down, so I held the back of a chair. I was sure Mother was going to die. Elizabeth was born with a long umbilical cord, which may be why she was immodest. They cut it short, though, so she'd be good and tight for her husband someday.

I pretended Elizabeth was my own. And when she got old enough, we went everywhere together. I wanted to protect her from dangerous things. Each time she tumbled, I was there to kiss the spot she bruised. I taught her which plants were safe to play with and which were not; where it was safe to go and where she should never stray. When she was older, our favorite thing was to play down at the river. One early summer day we were there and white clouds boiled up over the trees and the water was so blue I wanted to eat it. We took off our shoes and waded in. When we climbed out, Elizabeth knocked one of my shoes off the boulder where I'd left it and it splashed into the water. I lunged after it and snatched it from the current, but the leather was soaked through.

When we got home, I tried to tuck it behind my skirts but Father noticed and asked me what I was hiding. I produced the wet shoe. His face darkened and he demanded an explanation. A pinprick of spit hit my cheek when he shouted. He made the shoes himself! It was an accident, I insisted. We put our shoes carefully on the rock, but Betty slipped. He forbade me to wear shoes for the rest of the week, to learn, he said, more respect for my belongings and their value. Going to milk the cow was the worst torment. Large fists of thistle chewed my feet. By week's end, my feet were swollen, covered with cuts and scratches, nearly too sore to walk on. On Sabbath, I walked into meeting and people looked away. They would not interfere. They knew Father. After we returned from meeting, he gave me back my shoes. "I hope you've learned your lesson," he said.

You never knew what would set him off, when that dark cliff over his eyes would appear and he'd rage and hit Mother or one of us children. We wanted him happy but didn't know how to keep him that way. Sometimes he was happy. I was fearful of Father and would do anything to make him love me. The more he beat me, the harder I tried to please him. But Elizabeth, young, brave Elizabeth, could not accept Father's cruelty. She had the courage of an adult, not the humility of a child. She refused to do what she was told if she believed the demand unreasonable. Once when Father hit Mother, Elizabeth jumped on his back and pummeled her small fists into his shoulder. He laughed and shrugged her off, sliding her down to the floor. The most frightening encounter, though, was the day he nearly killed her for refusing to follow an order. Had Mother and I not run from the house as he walloped and kicked her, she would surely have expired. That was the only time I was able to save her.

Part of me hated her for her outspokenness, hated her for thinking she did not have to live by Father's rules, that she could make her own. I certainly had learned how to follow orders. Who did she think she was that she could live as she saw fit? But another part of me longed to be like her—bold enough to speak out though everyone instructed us to be silent.

Once, before Elizabeth was born, Father let me sit on his lap— I'm sure he didn't do this with all the others, but I was his first child—and he told me a story of England, of a warm day full of sun that touched the leaves on the big tree next to his house, and the wind moved each leaf so it was music made of light. There was a party where the boys and the girls played together, dressed in their finest clothes, and danced around a tree with ribbons. Then he grew stern. "But that was sinful," he said, straightening his legs and making me slide down. He left the house and didn't come back until we were all in bed, including Mother; I heard him climb in with her. The mattress crackled. He moaned some and breathed heavy as he must have mounted her and done his business. A few minutes later he snored deeply. In the middle of the night he relieved himself; the stream of piss hit the empty "hourglass" then strayed over the edge and hit the wood floor.

In the morning when I lifted it, the pot was sticky. I carried it to the edge of the woods behind the privy and tossed its contents. This was my daily job. In the frozen winter months, I couldn't cover the solid waste with a layer of soil and steam rose up in the cold air.

One summer day Father piled us all in the wagon and took us to Andover to the Flints' house where we were allowed to play in the cherry orchard. The branches drooped with fruit. Mother and Mrs. Flint spread a blanket on the ground and lay on their backs with their knees up. We climbed the ladder tipped against a tree and picked as many cherries as we could eat. After a while our fingers and mouths were dark red. I bit half a cherry, picked out the pit, and smeared it across Mother's lips to make her beautiful, I said. She smiled. We picked raspberries, too, though they were more difficult, the briars reaching at you like pricked arms, pesting your skirts and sleeves and leaving perforated, fiery lines of blood across your skin. Father stayed indoors all day in Mr. Flint's study and read to us from the Psalms at dusk when we all came in, our skin pink from the sun.

He used to lead us in prayer several times during the day. Upon rising. At the noon meal. Before bed. The words tumbled out of his mouth. He told me I would probably burn infinitely in hell but if I prayed hard and often enough, there was a chance I wouldn't. He said he and Mother were going to die and that we children must take care to guarantee our salvation. Every day when I woke up I wondered if they would still be alive. I was eight years old. I imagined a desert, a pile of sand, a bird taking one grain of sand every ten years: infinity. When Sara Whitaker died—she was only my age—Father said I, too, could die at any moment. Was I ready to meet my God? he queried. I was eating an apple at the time and I looked up from it and said yes, looked him right in the eye. But that night when we read Psalms I suddenly pictured my own death, my own rotten and putrid soul smeared like feces across the walls of hell. I began shaking, burst into tears, and wailed. No one could console me. My prayers felt like pieces of wood.

I must have been quite young the day I found Mother lying on the floor sobbing, for my head did not reach the edge of the eating board. She was lying underneath it and I crawled to her and wanted to make her happy again. I have since asked her about this but she says she doesn't remember. She was holding something made of glass in her hand. I believe it was broken and that is why she was crying. Perhaps I only dreamed it, but her grief is vivid as cherry-painted lips. In my memory her delicate hand cups something fragile and lost and I could not comfort her. Maybe it was not glass but something else my memory has transformed into glass, a letter, maybe, or a lace bonnet.

One day Elizabeth and I were walking home from the port where we'd been sent to buy fish and saw Goody Johnson sitting on the stone fence next to the cow pasture. Her shoulders were like heavy boulders. You could tell from her swollen eyes she had been crying. She had a branch of bittersweet in her hand that she kept turning like something with a broken neck. She couldn't see us and we could hear the crackle of the orange and red berries. She spoke to the cows in front of her in the pasture, shook the sprig of bittersweet at them as a mother does a spoon to a child who's misbehaving while she's cooking. She kept saying to the cows, "Never again. Never, do you hear?" Her voice was high as it is when you talk and cry at the same time. She finally stood up, rubbed her eyes with the back of her hands, and strode down the path that led to their house. I told Elizabeth that was a witch we'd just seen. We told Mother as soon as we came home.

Everybody saw witches everywhere. A neighbor dog jumped on a child's leg and started pumping and that was evidence. Someone walked by a pigpen and shooed them just for fun because pigs scare so easily and that was a sure sign. The widow Curtis was known as a potion doctress. She healed nearly everyone in the village at one time or another. When we had ailments, Mother took us to her house and she walked through her herb garden— the fists of herbs planted in orderly beds—and plucked something here, another thing there, then took the palmful of ingredients to the shed. She placed them in the stone mortar and crushed them together with the pestle, made a paste. She put this in a mug she filled with well water and added a spoon of sugar. Widow Curtis comforted many ailments—sometimes poison ivy—with a paste she'd make and pat on to the raw burning area.

Widow Curtis knew too much. She healed people, did God's work. She was one of the first to dangle on the green, the crisp soles of her boots at eye level a warning to all. It was the doctor who swore against her, worried she would take his patients away.

Mother had an herb garden. She used old dry bread and mixed it with sage and onion and mushrooms we collected in the woods. She mixed in drippings from yesterday's roast then pressed it into the cavity of a chicken or other game. She folded the legs together as if forcing the bird to pray, then wound the string around the ends, to hold it closed and keep its juices in.

She gave me some strong tea when I got my monthlies. I held my legs together tight, trying to keep my blood from escaping. It frightened me, seeing a puddle of clotted blood one day in my knickers. I hated myself for such vileness. I left the knickers on the ground next to the privy and went to find Mother. I pulled her to the spot and pointed. She looked and asked me did I know what it was. I had a vague idea from hearing girls talk that it was because in the night I was visited by a witch who cut me. Mother frowned and told me that it had nothing to do with witches. She explained to me it was because now I was able to have children. Of course, I lived in terror from that moment forward that at any time I could and would become pregnant. Each time I had my monthlies, it meant a baby had died in me and was dripping out.

Though I had loved the outdoors as a young child, as I grew older, I eventually grew to fear it. If I had counted the days to spring when I could wade in the river, by the time I was a young woman, I was more comfortable within the walls of the house than I was outdoors. Perhaps it was the minister's weekly evocation of the howling woods and their half-human, half-devil inhabitants that lay beyond our civilized, tamed corner. The savages, as he called them, stole Christian people from their homes, cut out their tongues from their heads and grilled and savored them for supper. Their appetites were voracious. They were creatures of the wild, and the wild was only as far away as the edge of our northwest field. Though for years the Indians had been friendly, coming and going into our town as they pleased, partaking in commerce with ease and courtesy, problems with them were now becoming worse. Every year there were a few more men and their wives who built a house in the woods. The Indians appeared at the edge of the forest and watched, devils that they were. One area to the west was already nicely cleared. Someone built a house there, and no sooner had it been built than an Indian claimed it was on his hunting ground.

It was about that time the women of Marblehead killed the two Indians. Felicity Whitburn, having married a man from that town, was visiting her parents in Haverhill and told me the story. The Indians had pirated some boats near there and were captured and brought to Marblehead. They were to be handed over to the constable and taken to court in Boston. There had been many raids that year and the women were afraid to sleep in their own houses. Not satisfied the savages would get what they deserved, the women descended on the port.

"I grabbed some stones next to the marsh," said Felicity, "and handed some around. Others grabbed large pieces of wood from woodpiles," she continued. "We sent the Englishmen off, beating them with the sticks, and threatening them with the rocks, as they would protect the swarthy heathens."

I was struck by Felicity's calm voice as she told me the story. She stared off over the water as she spoke, then turned her head toward me. "As we gathered around the two Indian men," she said, "I could smell their fear, stronger than the salt air. One of them was old and bent at the knee. He looked me right in the eye. The other was our age. We went at them, smashing as hard as we could, and soon made jelly of them. Someone started tearing at the red flesh and soon we all were pulling it from their bones with our fingers. Charity produced a knife and carved off their heads. We carried them to the dock and dumped them in the water. The blood blossomed and the marsh grass scratched the June night. Lightning bugs were just starting to appear."

I was appalled at her gruesome poetry, at the revolting account, but knew as well as anyone these devils needed to be wiped out.

One incident after another with the Indians occurred and eventually every able-bodied man in Haverhill was given a gun and plenty of ammunition. One of these men was Thomas, whom I'd first seen at a town meeting where the eldermen were deciding what to do about the Indian problem. (Though of course we were not allowed to say anything, women could go and listen at meetings.) It was February and the room was close, the air thick with smoke and the odor of so many bodies. The people in that room were nervous about the situation and the air stank of it. The men decided that the meeting house should be fortified—they would put in portholes and strengthen the walls. They would burn the old brush and top wood on the common so as to remove any hiding places. After the meeting ended, as I was dragging my heavy skirts across the snow, Thomas Dustin came up to me and asked me was I afraid of the Indians. I said of course I was, as any Christian soul might be, except those praying Indians who had allowed themselves to be educated and see the proper way to live. "Did you see the one who dumped his basket of fish on the common a few weeks back?" he asked.

I did not, I answered, but of course we'd all heard of it.

John Littleale passed by us and nodded a greeting. He was a silent man. From a family of thirteen children, Littleale had decided to live on his own in the woods, undoubtedly up to something evil. The town countenanced it for some time, but finally ordered him to move into town and live with a family or be sent to labor in a prison in Hampton.

As I walked home I decided Thomas Dustin would be as good a husband as any and if what he was aiming toward was me for a wife I was not against the notion. He courted me for several months, whispering when we were together, as if the things he had to tell me about our future life together were so gorgeous, so precious and exquisite, that to say them too loud would taint them. He had just claimed a track of land in the wilderness about two miles out from the common and needed me to live there with him. My only hesitation was it meant living in the wild. I would be an hour's walk from my family and would only see them occasionally. Worst of all, we would be in the howling, prowling wild, where every leaf's movement suggested a heathen was hiding, lurking, staring out at us. The vulgar people were known to lurk and spy.

We were married the following year.

ANNE FINGER

Comrade Luxemburg and Comrade Gramsci Pass Each Other at a Congress of the Second International in Switzerland on the 10th of March, 1912

NOTE: *Italicized sections of the text are quotations from Johann Goethe, Rosa Luxemburg, Johnny Cash, Alfred Döblin, Antonio Gramsci, Vladimir Lenin, Benito Mussolini, Adolf Hitler, Karl Koch, and the Bible.*

It never happened.
It could not have happened.

It could not have happened that at a crowded congress of the Second International held in a resort hotel on the shores of Lake Catano in the foothills of the Swiss Alps, alongside a snow-fed lake with waters of such pure, crystalline blue that even in the very center one could peer straight down and clearly see the fluid shadows of the waters' ripples speckling the rocks at the bottom, the delegates from the socialist parties of the world gathering in clots in the hallways, doing the real business of the congress there, with urgent imprecations, hands grasping forearms, voices dropped almost to whispers and glances over their shoulders, while upstairs an overworked chambermaid with varicose veins, Madame Robert, flicked a sheet in the air, sending motes of dust dancing in the afternoon sunshine, that Comrade Rosa Luxemburg and Comrade Antonio Gramsci limped past each other.

It never happened that Luxemburg, who had been detained after her speech by those anxious to get her advice, to give her theirs, to merely say that they had spoken with her, yes, *individually, personally,* at last signaled to her companion with her eyes, who worked his way through the knot of people surrounding her, laid a paternal hand on her arm, said, "Rosa, you must..." and Rosa allowed herself to be led away, departing the Geneva Room at 2:52 in the afternoon, while at 2:51 Comrade Gramsci had sneezed, futilely searched his pockets for a handkerchief, and, having wiped his nose surreptitiously with the back of his hand, bowed his head and hurried through the crowded corridor to

ascend to his room on the fifth floor to fetch one, so that, two-thirds of the way along, the two of you would pass each other.
No, it could not have happened.

On March 10, 1912, at eight minutes to three in the afternoon, Rosa Luxemburg was in her apartment on Lindenstrasse in Berlin, preparing a lecture for the Party School, thumbing through Goethe's *Faust,* looking for the quotation *No one yields empire / To another; no one will yield it who has gained it by force...,* the same volume that she will drop into her purse when she hears the footsteps coming up the stairs of the house in Neukölln to take her to her death six years later; and Gramsci was a twenty-one-year-old, a poverty-stricken Sardinian student eating his first meal in three days, a plate of *spaghetti con olio,* at a trattoria on the Via Pereigia in Turin, reading a linguistics text as he ate, at a table just a little bit too high for him, so that his arms ached slightly from the odd angle at which they had to be maneuvered. At the next table a father moaned and patted his belly, pushed his chair back from the table, then urged his plump daughters to eat dessert, accompanying his coaxings with tugs at their flesh, they were too thin, altogether too thin, his dumplings, his darlings. The coy daughters protested; the *padre* signaled the waiter to clear away the platters of calamari and pasta, the remains of the spring lamb, the half-flask of wine. Later, limping home alone in a sharp wind with his half-empty belly (why does one feel the cold so much more when one is hungry?), Gramsci tried to name the force that allowed him to watch the remains of the rich man's dinner being taken away while he still hungered: a dog, a dumb brute, would have leapt for it, seized the lamb in his teeth. The dog would have been a better socialist than I am, he thought.

No, Comrade Luxemburg does not pass Comrade Gramsci as she heads down the corridor, on her way to sit next to Karl Liebknecht at dinner, on her way to dine with him and twelve Judases, on her way to *the unprecedented, the incredible 4th of August, 1914,* when the men she thought of as her comrades will vote for war appropriations, so that the workers of Germany can kill and in turn be killed by the workers of Italy and France and England; on her way to the gloomy evening a few weeks later when she and Clara Zetkin will sit in her parlor, four feet in scuffed slippers resting on the fender before the fire, debating, not the woman question, not organizational questions of the party, but whether laudanum or prussic acid would be a better way to go: because *mass murder has become a boring monotonous daily business;* on her way to listening to the whistle of the 3:19 train carrying Mathilde away from her, in the prison where she was locked up for her opposition to the war (*If they freed me from this prison / if that railroad train was mine / you bet I'd move it on / a little further down the line / far from Folsom Prison . . .*); she will promise Sonja Liebknecht to go to Corsica with her after the war (*On high, nothing except barren rock formations which are a noble grey; below, luxuriant olive trees, cherry trees, and age-old chestnut trees. And above everything, a prehistoric quiet—no human voices, no bird calls, only a stream rippling somewhere between rocks, or the wind on high whispering between the cliffs—still the same wind that swelled Ulysses' sails . . .*), but she will never see Corsica again; instead she will spend her first night of freedom, a sleepless night, at the railway workers' union hall, preparing for a demonstration the next day; on her way to Berlin where red flags will be flying everywhere, *precisely when on the surface everything seems hopeless and miserable, a complete change is getting ready . . .* ; on her way to her dazed, lurching walk through the corridors of the Hotel Eden (*You know I really hope to die at my post, in a street fight or in prison*), past the chambermaids and valets who, a few weeks previously, might have joined the throngs in the streets of Berlin, might even have had a sister or brother who took part in the occupation of the *Vorwärts* building, demanding of a newcomer, "*Why have you come so late? And why have you not brought others with you?,*" who will now join in the jeering: Jew, sow, red whore, cripple, Jew; on her way to the black car, on her way to the bullet to her brain that pierces her left temporal lobe and wipes out the throne within her brain where reason sat; on her way to becoming, for a few brief minutes, no longer Dr. Luxemburg, no longer the visionary, the prophet, just a body, an unconscious (. . . *sometimes it seems to me that I am not really a human being at all, but rather a bird or a beast in human form . . .*); a body whose dead weight will plummet into the waters of the Landwehr Canal.

She does not pass Comrade Gramsci, on his way to his room

on the fifth floor to fetch a handkerchief; on his way to the Petrograd train station, where he will be met by a delegation of four men and one woman, who will stand on the platform scanning the air above him, and he will pretend not to notice the few seconds' lag after he announces himself, in a voice he has made as deep as possible (this shrunken hunchback, the famous leader?—sometimes they will have been warned ahead of time, that he is *handicapped, deformed,* but then they will expect some Cyclops, a Minotaur, not this limping dwarf); on his way to being led into the courtroom where everyone save the prisoners will appear in tragicomic fascist splendor, a double cordon of militiamen in plumed black helmets, heels of well-polished shoes clicked together, backs straight, an emblematic dagger poised in an identical position in the belt of each one, the marshalls bearing standards that will read SPQR, Senatus Populusque Romanarum—of course, this will recall to him Marx's comment about history repeating itself, the first time as tragedy and the second as farce; he will limp in dirty, unshaven, feeling like a wounded, crawling animal: a ferret, perhaps, slithering and predatory; he will feel a sense of physical shame, and understand again a sentence he will have written years before, when the Turin workers' councils failed: *the bourgeoisie lies in ambush in the hearts of the proletariat;* on his way to becoming the great mind, the Gramsci who floats, a head without a body, on fading posters thumbtacked to apartment walls in Madison, Wisconsin, and Berkeley, California.

Rosa, you warned us, *we can no more skip a period in our historical development than a man can jump over his shadow.* But still I spray-paint on the walls of the Hotel Leveque a slogan that won't be heard for fifty-odd years hence: "All power to the imagination!" I imagine that in those days when we didn't yet have a name for ourselves, when the only words were *handicapped, lame, deformed, hunchback, dwarf, cripple,* when the only words were silence, that we could speak.

I imagine that Comrade Luxemburg stares, looks away, but then laughs at herself for doing so: not out loud, not a full-throated, rich deep laugh, but only a laugh of mild amusement at her "instinctive" reaction. And then she turns, smiles, as you or I might do, passing each other in the corridor at a meeting filled with ABs.

She stops, stretches out her hand, says, "We haven't met. I'm Rosa Luxemburg."

"Of course," he mutters, "yes, of course," stretching out his hand in return, conscious of the fact that it's the one he used in the absence of a handkerchief.

"And you?" she says, helping out the flustered young man. He gives his name. "Let's talk," she says.

After dinner, when the coffee's served, they meet out on the verandah. Of course, the stone benches out there are backless, and so they'll schlepp three chairs out—one to prop their feet on, which otherwise would dangle above the ground.

"So," Rosa asks right out, "has your disability made difficulties for you, in the party?"

Antonio shrugs. "They—the workers—trust me."

She nods, she knows. The wound on the outside, so that strangers on a train pick you to tell their tale to.

"But they fear it, too," she supplies.

"Yes, they fear it, too."

"And yet," she says, "I often wonder if I would have got as far in the party as I have if it weren't for—"

"The de-sexualization."

"De-gendering was more what I was going to say," she says. Because of all those years of her growing up when it seemed that she was destined to be permanently outside the realm of desire, his words make her a bit prickly. If she were honest with herself about this—although she couldn't be—she'd admit that it was one of the things that led her to socialism: that it was the place where her strength of mind, of character, could overcome her physical flaw, allow her to be desired. She only lets herself know that she felt freedom here, a freedom she couldn't feel anywhere else.

Comrades, I want you to go on but this conversation has grown awkward, studded with anachronisms, impossible to write. All power to the imagination? As difficult a slogan to put into practice as *All power to the soviets*.

And although I want to holler back through time, "Please, speak to each other," I cannot let you know what's to come. Mussolini is not yet a fascist, he has not yet become a man of steel, a man who will slap cold water on raw morning flesh, his chest puffed out like an enormous steam engine; *the masses are a woman,* he will say, and, at a certain moment, when, haranguing them from a balcony, he feels their submissive spirit reach up towards him, he will strip off his shirt to show those muscles like iron bands, jut forward that great leonine head, the lumpishness of his bald skull giving the effect of a Roman head chiseled in marble. Hitler is still nothing more than a gleam in the evil eye of history. He has not yet spun that web of propaganda where disease, prostitution, the caftaned Jew lurking in the alley waiting to defile the Aryan woman, *the suffocating perfume of our modern eroticism,* the degenerates contaminating the healthy and passing on their defective genes to their offspring, blur together and become one. He has not yet declared that Germany must become a healthy state. Kommandant Koch of Buchenwald has not yet said, *There are no sick men in my camp. They are all either well or dead.* Mussolini, Hitler, Koch, will understand: the worship of the healthy body, the fear of us, is the taproot of fascism.

But Rosa, sober Rosa, leans forward through time and reprimands me: *In the beginning was the act.* No, they can't yet speak to each other. We don't yet exist. We are the sons and daughters of fascism, as well as the daughters and sons of ourselves.

So I try again. I fast-forward through the next four bloody years of history: the soldiers look like Keystone Kops as they rush out of their trenches, grimace, fall to the ground, and the next wave of soldiers rises, and does the same, and the next does the same, and the next does the same and the next does the same and the next does the same, until some twenty-two million have died and I hit the "play" button and return to normal speed.

Rosa walks out the doors of Breslau Prison, she speaks at the rally in Berlin, she writes, *There is order in Berlin . . . your order is built on sand.* But she never takes that last dazed, lurching walk through the corridors of the Hotel Eden, she never is found, a bloated marshmallow of a corpse, eyeless, bobbing against the locks of the Landwehr Canal. Instead she escapes to the Soviet Union, from there she hopscotches to New York. Antonio, at first I imagine that you were persuaded to leave Italy before your arrest, but even in the world of the imagination, I can't wish *The Prison Notebooks*, the *Letters*, out of existence. Forgive me, Nino, but I am sending you into that first filthy cell in Regina Coeli Prison, where the single bare bulb burns all night long, and the lice scuttle through the mattress; and into all the prison cells that followed that one. Let's suppose that Romain Rolland, who has worked so diligently for your release all these years—circulating petitions, writing endless letters, lobbying in the court of world opinion—despairs of those tactics: instead, knowing how close you are to death, he organizes a commando raid against the Quisisana Clinic. Chuck Norris is the advance man, he disguises himself as a taciturn (male) nurse, we'll explain away his fair complexion by having him pretend to be German; at the appointed hour, while a helicopter lowers itself towards the roof, he'll pick you up in his arms like a baby (you weighed only forty-two kilograms then), toss you over his shoulder, and, a machine gun in his free hand, take out a few fascists as he rushes to the roof. Chuck will cradle you in his arms, stroke your black hair away from your hot forehead, say, "Hey, guy, it's okay. You're all right, comrade." There will be no flier headlined "Italian Fascism Has Murdered Gramsci." No, comrade, you will live.

Neither of you will become famous. Sorry, there's truth to that old saw about death being good for your career. Rosa ends up giving lectures at the New School, writing for magazines with ever-dwindling circulations. She began her article "Either/Or" with a quote from Revelations: *I would thou wert cold or hot. So then because thou art lukewarm, and neither cold nor hot, I will spew thee out of my mouth.* But now the masses have moved to White Plains, they drive DeSotos, she has become an apocalyptic crank. Antonio sits out the war years in the warm dry air of Southern California, regaining some measure of health, joining up with that colony of squabbling, quibbling, squalling leftist exiles.

What will I do with them, now that I've saved them? Have them meet again, on a subway platform in Brooklyn; Rosa, 103, with that papery, almost smooth-as-a-baby's patch of skin on her cheeks that old, old women get; and Antonio, in his eighties, lumbering and wheezing up the steps. But then, it could only be the early seventies: too early, still. No, I'll have time pass, but the two of them stay in their late forties, the ages they were when they died; it's 1990, Rosa is sitting on the bench at Ditmas station in Brooklyn, waiting for the F train, the Americans with Disabilities Act has just passed, she's reading the article about it in *The New York Times.* Antonio comes and sits down next to her. He knows enough to leave a couple of New York inches between the two of them, but still she sidles a bit away. He can't help looking over her shoulder, reading the same article she is. She shakes the newspaper a bit, casts him a quick cold glance. He looks away; but then she says, "Excuse me. We've met, haven't we?"

What shall I have the two of them say? Shall I have Antonio say that our movement must concern itself with more than legislation, *must reach for the solution to more complex tasks than those proposed by the present development of the struggle; namely, for the creation of a new, integral culture...*; shall I have Rosa come back with the necessity of our movement being democratic, that we must make our own errors, *errors... infinitely more fruitful and more valuable than the infallibility* of any CIL board and all its high-powered consultants?

But no, it's another conversation I can't imagine.

No, I have to go back to that hotel corridor.

Although it could not have happened that on the 10th of March, 1912, at a congress of the Second International, in a corridor of the Hotel Leveque, at precisely 2:53, that Comrade Luxemburg, heading in a southerly direction down the corridor towards the dining hall while Comrade Gramsci headed towards the north staircase, passed each other, still, had it happened, Rosa would have startled slightly as she glimpsed him, the misshapen dwarf limping towards her in a secondhand black suit so worn the fabric is turning green with age, her eye immediately drawn to this disruption in the visual field. Realizing she was staring, she would have glanced quickly away. And then, the moment after, realizing that the quick aversion of the gaze was as much of an insult as the stare, she would have turned her head back, but tried to make her gaze general. Comrade Rosa would have felt a slight flicker of embarrassment? shame? revulsion? dread? a feeling that can have no name?

Would Gramsci at first have bowed his head in shame, then

raised his head, stared back, deciding that her right to look at him equaled his right to look at her? Did a slight smile pass across his face because he was glad to know that such a prominent comrade shared his condition?

It is all over in a matter of seconds.

But this never happened, and even if it had, it would not have mattered. What passed between the two of you belongs to the realm of thought before speech, of the shape of the future before it can be seen: a nameless discomfort, not yet even a premonition.

No, there is no such place on earth. You will not find this Lake Catano on any map: I have created it out of words. This congress never happened; the two of you were not there.

Look down through those clear blue waters of Lake Catano to the shifting shadows of the lake's ripples that speckle the rocks at the bottom; see the shadows grow larger and larger until they dissolve into nothingness; now the lake itself, which never existed, disappears. The scullery girl chopping onions in the kitchen automatically wipes her cheeks with the backs of her hands, and discovers that her cheeks are not wet with onion tears; surprised, she sniffs the air: it does not smell of onions, it does not smell of anything. Upstairs, the chambermaid, old Madame Robert, stands on her aching legs and snaps a freshly laundered sheet through the air. Madame Robert, your legs will ache no more: I am writing away your pain, I am writing away your very existence. For a moment, the motes of dust you have disturbed dance glistening in the air, but then they cease, and first the sheet itself and then you yourself turn to shadows and vanish.

Issues of Appropriation

Penn Station, March 1991

I've been homeless down here so long

I didn't give up the worship of Jesus

Now I got my own room but it's not in my apartment

And God is a good god

And children if you're on that crack don't get addicted

Because me I waited too long and I'm itching all over every day

But if you get with Jesus he'll stay on you

Talk about Jesus to the children 'cause they'll be running the world

I should know nineteen brothers and sisters

How women could help me? *laughing* I found it out after all these years I come to find out I'm bisexual

More laughing

Practical ways well I want to learn how to speak Spanish oh I could've had a good job this morning but I didn't speak enough Spanish ain't that something?

Then my hands see how big they are? they won't even give me a job nobody

And I only get a check once a month and my rent is too high

But my social worker says she's going to help me find a place

I go in the hospital Monday to detox yeah

November 14 1989 they put a plug in my door and didn't even take me to court

On the hospital ward and when I went home with my key it wouldn't even go in the lock

Every man I had I found out they liked men

That's why I'm telling you I don't want any more men

I've known men and they've been very nice and then I found out they had their own lovers

Never been pregnant thank you Jesus

Seven years addicted to crack

I'm on the methadone and the methadone used to make me itchy all over so I started smoking

I used to forget to pick up my medicine

So they detoxed me

On meth for twenty-seven years and they detoxed me in two weeks

It was too fast

Now I feel myself deteriorating

I was two hundred pounds in May 1989 I weigh myself now I'm not even one hundred twenty-five

I never really told nobody the truth because I was ashamed of being on it

But I revealed it to my medical doctor and he said I only have one lung left that's functioning

So I've got to stop

I'm afraid then I'll find out I have the AIDS

He told me I don't have the AIDS

He told me my test came back HIV-positive virus

So I guess that's what I got the virus

I tried to kill myself

I took an overdose of pills

I didn't want to live with myself to know that another man was with another man

My medical doctor gave me something

My girlfriend said don't take it because they're just experimenting on you it'll give you cancer

So I'm not

Maybe you can help me contact someone

Because I don't want to die

I'm so young sixty-three it's young

I can't go to my brothers and sisters

Back home my key wouldn't fit in the lock

Issues of Appropriation, 2

Her name was Henrietta. She spoke into our tape recorder. I held the microphone. Ellen asked the questions. We spoke to other women that afternoon—in Penn Station, at Port Authority, at a Manhattan shelter, and a few days later at a shelter in the Bronx, where we sponsored a reception for a delegation of women for peace from various countries in the Middle East. It was March 1991. You remember, the Gulf War. The brief electrifying return of moral clarity, mass mobilization, gearing up for a long, indefinite season of protest, insurrection in the air.

All but two of the women doing this work were white. Most of the women on the street and in the shelters were black, and in the Bronx shelter, the better-funded shelter, a few were Latina. We were collecting homeless women's voices. This was a project, part of a larger project that was part of a larger project still: we had organized a women's fair to bring together in one church basement all the women's organizations serving the homeless and raped and battered women of New York City. (I say "we" about all this, so let me be clear: I was one of many, anything but a leader, more tentative than the leader, a participant learning as I went along.) One of our group would edit our tape of voices to accompany a slide show of photographs that another of our group was taking at the shelters and on the streets. The whole slide show/tape thing would be a powerfully constructed, collectively generated art object and take maybe five minutes to open our gathering of women. Other art moments would follow, as well as a variety of personal testimonials, but the main work of the evening would be the exchange of organizational information around the tables set up by the many participating groups. There would be an emphasis on empowerment.

Okay, so you get the idea. Let's go back to Penn Station.

The women were willing to talk to us. They didn't hold our
whiteness or our tape recorder against us (or not out loud). They
didn't care that we took a little moment of their lives away with
us. They wanted the sandwiches and cookies and apples we
offered them. They wanted our attention. They wanted us to listen. They wanted to be heard. They wanted us (and you) to sit
down and talk to them, to hear their stories, to know how they
got to where they got to be, each in her particular way. Not one of
them said, *Get out of my face, bitch,* or *Who are you, white girls, to
take, to tell my story? Who to?* or *Why?*

Still, when I listen to the tapes, there are moments that make me
uneasy. Consider this: Ellen is talking to a woman in the midtown
shelter. The woman answers a question about how the shelter
works for her, says the shelter meets her basic needs but they want
to move her to another. It all depends on who the shelter director
likes, she says. Since she's on medication, they just want to move
her out. Ellen asks if anyone really sees her. The woman doesn't
understand the question. Ellen amplifies: Who you are, you, your
own particular person. No, the woman says, no one does. Then
Ellen asks what women could do to help make that possible, to
help her to be seen, and the woman answers, thoughtfully and as if
with a shrug (as if I can hear a shrug in the tape-recorded silence):
Sit down and talk with me. A pause follows, then Ellen says, *That's
great. That's good. Let's end it right there.*

To be fair, Ellen didn't mean this as coldly as it sounds. She had a
relationship with the women at this shelter, maybe even with this
woman, had come to this shelter twice a week for years, counts
among her friends women she helped get off the street. Still, at
this distance, with only the tape to go on, the abrupt if warm dismissal is all I really hear.

What is the place, then, for witness, for gathering the stories, the
images, the words, and bringing them into the living rooms and

church basements, classrooms, lecture halls, movie theaters, galleries, museums, libraries, coffeehouses, and every other venue where *homed* people gather themselves in safety to encounter the rest of the world? I want to know how we are going to talk about the racialization of poverty in this country, especially gendered poverty, women's poverty, if, because her situation fits a stereotype (to return to Penn Station), we will not talk about Henrietta. We, too, fit a stereotype with our tape recorder and our sandwiches and our outrage and concern. Does that mean we should be silent and inactive? I won't say so.

At what moment does the issue of appropriation arise? (Homeless women, too, were present at our gathering, and formerly homeless women, battered white women, and white women suing their fathers twenty years later for rape.) At what moment does a problematic of representation become the issue rather than Henrietta herself? (And in whose interest?) Henrietta, who, chances are, if in 1991 she was sixty-three and homeless and HIV-positive and too scared to take her medication and had one good lung left from crack addiction, even if she detoxed, by now, chances are, is dead: Henrietta, with whom not one of us spoke again.

DIANA GARCÍA

Cotton Rows, Cotton Blankets

Sprawled on the back of a flatbed truck
we cradled hoes, our minds parceling rows
of cotton to be chopped by noon. Dawn stuck
in the air. Blackbirds rang the willows.

Ahead, a horse trailer stretched across the road.
Braced by youth and lengths of summer breeze
we didn't give a damn. We'd be late, we joked,
stalled by a pregnant mare draped in sheets.

Later, backs to the sun, bandannas tied
to shade our brows, hands laced with tiny cuts;
later, when the labor contractor
worked us through lunch without water; our dried
tongues cursed that mare in cotton blankets
brought to foal in the outlines of summer.

City Life

Peter had always been more than thoughtful in not pressing her about her past, and Beatrice was sure it was a reason for her choice of him. Most men, coming of age in a time that extolled openness and disclosure, would have thought themselves remiss in questioning her so little. Perhaps because he was a New Englander—one of four sons in a family that had been stable for generations—perhaps because he was a mathematician, perhaps because both the sight of her and her way of living had pleased him from the first and continued to please him, he had been satisfied with what she was willing to tell. "My parents are dead. We lived in Western New York State, near Rochester. I am an only child. I have no family left."

She preferred saying "I have no family left"—creating with her words an absence, a darkness, rather than to say what had been there, what she had ruthlessly left, with a ruthlessness that would have shocked anyone who knew her later. She had left them so thoroughly that she really didn't know if they were still living. When she tried to locate them, with her marriage and her children and the warm weight of her domestic safety at her back, there was no trace of them. It had shocked and frightened her how completely they had failed to leave a trace. This was the sort of thing most people didn't think of: how possible it was for people like her parents to impress themselves so little on the surface, the many surfaces of the world, that they would leave it or inhabit it with the same lack of a mark.

They were horrors, her parents, the sort people wanted to avert their eyes from, that people felt it was healthful to avert their eyes from. They had let their lives slip very far, further than anyone Beatrice now knew could even begin to imagine. But it had always been like that: a slippage so continuous that there was simultaneously a sense of slippage and of already having slipped.

It was terribly clear to her. She was brought up in filth. Most people, Beatrice knew, believed that filth was temporary, one of those things, unlike disease or insanity or social hatred—that didn't root itself in but was an affair of surfaces, therefore dislodgeable by effort, will, and the meagerest brand of intelligence. That was, Beatrice knew, because people didn't understand filth. They mistook its historical ordinariness for simplicity. They didn't understand the way it could invade and settle, take over, dominate, and for good, until it became, inevitably, the only true thing about a place and the only lives that could be lived there. Dust, grime, the grease of foods, the residues of bodies, the smells that lived in the air, palpable, malign, unidentifiable, impossible to differentiate: an ugly population of refugees from an unknowable location, permanent, stubborn, knife-faced settlers who had right of occupancy—the place was theirs now—and would never leave.

Beatrice's parents had money for food, and the rent must have been paid to someone. They had always lived in the one house: her mother, her father, and herself. Who could have owned it? Who would have put money down for such a place? One-story, nearly windowless, the outside walls made of soft shingle in the semblance of pinkish gray brick. It must have been built from the first entirely without love, with the most cynical understanding, Beatrice had always thought, of the human need for shelter and the dollar value that it could bring. Everything was cheap and thin, done with the minimum of expense and of attention. No thought was given to ornament or amplitude, or even to the long, practical run: what wouldn't age horribly or crumble, splinter, quickly fade.

As she grew older, she believed the house had been built to hide some sort of criminality. It was in the middle of the woods, down a dirt road half a mile down Highway 117, which led nowhere she knew, or maybe south, she somehow thought, to Pennsylvania. Her parents said it had once been a hunting lodge, but she didn't believe it. When she was old enough to have learned about bootlegging, and knew that whiskey had been smuggled in from Canada, she was convinced that the house had had something to do with that. She could always imagine petty gangsters, local thugs in mean felt hats and thin-soled shoes trading liquor for money, throwing their cigarette butts down on the hard, infertile ground, then driving away from the house, not giving it a thought until it was time for their next deal.

Sometimes she thought it was the long periods of uninhabited-ness that gave the house its closed, and vengeful, character. But when she began to think like that, it wasn't long before she under-stood that kind of thought to be fantastical. It wasn't the house, houses had no will or nature. Her parents had natures, and it was their lives and the way they lived that made their dwelling a mon-strosity.

She had awakened each day in dread, afraid to open her eyes, knowing the first thing they fell on would be ugly. She didn't even know where she could get something for herself that might be beautiful. The word couldn't have formed itself in her mind in any way that could attach to an object that was familiar to her, or that she could even imagine having access to. She heard, as if from a great distance, people using the word "beautiful" in rela-tion to things like trees or sunsets, but her faculty for understand-ing things like this had been so crippled that the attempt to comprehend what people were saying when they spoke like this filled her with a kind of panic. She couldn't call up even the first step that would allow her, even in the far future, to come close to what they meant. They were talking about things out of doors when they talked about trees and sunsets. And what was the good of that? You could go out of doors. The blueness of the sky, the brightness of the sun, the freshness of a tree would greet you, but in the end you would only have to go back somewhere to sleep. And that would not be beautiful; it would be where you lived. So beauty seemed a dangerous, foreign, and irrelevant idea. She turned for solace, not to it, but to the nature of enclosure. Every-thing in her life strained toward the ideal of separations: how to keep the horror of her parents' life from everything that could be called her life.

She learned what it was she wanted from watching her grade school teachers cutting simple shapes—squares, triangles—and writing numbers in straight columns on the blackboard or on paper with crisp, straight blue lines. The whiteness of pages, the unmuddled black of print, struck her as desirable; the dry rasping of the scissors, the click of a stapler, the riffling of a rubber band around a set of children's tests. She understood all these things as prosperity, and knew that her family was not prosperous; they were poor. But she knew as well that their real affliction wasn't poverty but something different—you might, perhaps, say worse—but not connected to money. If she could have pointed to that—a simple lack of money—it would have been more hopeful for her. But she knew it wasn't poverty that was the problem. It was the way her parents were. It was what they did.

They drank. That was what they did. It was, properly speaking, the only thing they did. But no, she always told herself when she began to think that way, it wasn't the only thing. Her father, after all, had gone out to work. He was a gravedigger in a Catholic cemetery. Each morning he woke in the dark house. Massive, nearly toothless, and still in his underwear, he drank black coffee with a shot in it for breakfast, and then put on his dark-olive work pants and shirts, his heavy boots—in winter a fleece-lined coat and cap—and started the reluctant car driving down the dirt road. He came home at night, with a clutch of bottles in a paper bag, to begin drinking. He wasn't violent or abusive; he was interested only in the stupor he could enter and inhabit. This, Beatrice knew early on, was his true home.

Her mother woke late, her hair in pin curls wrapped in a kerchief, which she rarely bothered to undo. She was skeletally thin; her skin was always in a state of dull eruptions; red spidery veins on her legs always seemed to Beatrice to be the tracks of a slow disease. Just out of bed, she poured herself a drink, not bothering to hide it in coffee, and drank it from a glass that had held cheese spread mixed with pimentos, which her parents ate on crackers when they drank, and which was often Beatrice's supper. Beatrice's mother would sit for a while on the plaid couch, watch television, then go back to bed. The house was nearly always silent; there were as few words in the house as there were ornaments. It was another reason Peter liked her. She had a gift, he said, for silence, a gift he respected, that he said too few people had. She wondered if he would have prized this treasure if he'd known its provenance.

Beatrice saw everything her parents did because she slept in the large room. When she was born, her parents had put a crib for her in the corner of the room nearest their bedroom, opposite the wall where the sink, the stove, and the refrigerator were. It didn't occur to them that she might want privacy; when she grew taller, they replaced her crib with a bed, but they never imagined she had any more rights or desires than an infant. The torpor, the disorder of their lives, spread into her quarters. For years, it anguished her to see their slippers, their half-read newspapers, broken bobby pins, half-empty glasses, butt-filled ashtrays traveling like bacilli into the area she thought of as hers. When she was ten, she bought some clothesline and some tacks. She bought an Indian bedspread from a hippie store in town; rose-colored, with a print of tigers; the only vivid thing in the place. She made a barrier between herself and them. Her father said something unkind about it, but she took no notice.

For the six years after that, she came home as little as she could, staying in the school library until it closed, walking home miles in the darkness. She sat on her bed, did what was left of her homework, and, as early as possible, lay down to sleep. At sunrise, she would leave the house, walking the roads till something opened in the town—the library, the five-and-ten, the luncheonette—then walking for more hours till the sun set. She didn't love the woods; she didn't think of them as nature, with all the implications she had read about. But they were someplace she could be until she had no choice but to be *there* again, but not quite *there,* not in the place that was *theirs,* but her place, behind her curtain, where she needn't see the way they lived.

She moved out of her parents' house two days after she graduated from high school. She packed her few things and moved to Buffalo, where she got a job in a tool and die factory, took night courses at the community college. She did this for five years, then took all her savings and enrolled in the elementary education program at the University of Buffalo full time. She'd planned it all out carefully, in her tiny room, living on yogurt she made from powdered milk, allowing it to ferment in a series of thermoses she'd bought at garage sales, eating the good parts of half-rotten fruit and vegetables she'd bought for pennies, the fresh middle parts of loaves of day-old bread. Never, in those years, did she buy a new blouse or skirt or pair of jeans. She got her clothes from the Salvation Army; it was only later, after she married, that she learned to sew.

In her second semester, she met Peter in a very large class: European History 1789–1945. He said he'd fallen in love with several things about her almost at once: the look of her notebooks, the brilliant white of the collar of her shirt as it peeked over the top of her pastel-blue Shetland sweater, the sheer pink curves of her fingernails. He said he'd been particularly taken by her thumb. Most women's thumbs were ugly and betrayed the incompleteness of their femininity, the essential coarseness of it. The fineness of her thumb, the way the nail curved and was placed within the flesh, showed there wasn't a trace of coarseness in her: everything connected with her was, and would always be, fine. He didn't find out until they'd dated a few times that she was older, more than three years older than he was. He accepted that she'd had to work those years because her parents had—tragically—died.

Beatrice knew what Peter saw when he looked at her: clarity and simplicity and thrift, an almost holy sign of order, a plain creature without hidden parts or edges, who would sail through life before him making a path through murky seas, leaving to him plain sailing: nothing in the world to obstruct him or the free play of his mind. She knew that he didn't realize that he had picked her in part for the emptiness of her past, imagining a beautiful blankness, blameless, unpopulated, clear. His pity for her increased her value for him: she was an exile in the ordinary world he was born into, lacking the encumbrances that could make for problems in his life. He believed that life could be simple, that he would leave from a cloudless day and drop into the teeming fog of mathematics, which for him was peopled, creatured, a tumultuous society he had to colonize and civilize and rule.

She knew he felt he could leave all the rest to her, turning to her at night with the anomaly of his ardor, another equation she could elegantly solve. His curiosity about the shape of her desire was as tenderly blunted as his curiosity about her past, and she was as glad of the one as of the other. Making love to him, an occurrence she found surprisingly frequent, she could pretend she was sitting through a violent and fascinating storm that certainly would pass. Having got through it, she could be covered over in grateful tenderness for the life that he made possible: a life of clean linen and bright rooms, of matched dishes and a variety of specialized kitchen items: each unique, for one use only, and not, as everything in her mother's house was, interchangeable.

So the children came, three boys, and then the farmhouse, bought as a wreck, transformed by Beatrice Talbot into a treasure, something acquaintances came to see as much (more, she thought, if they were honest) as they did the family itself. Then Peter's tenure, and additions on the house: a sewing room, a greenhouse, then uncovering the old woodwork, searching out antique stores, auctions, flea markets for the right furniture—all this researched in the university library and in the local library— and the children growing and needing care so that by the time Peter came home with the news that was the first breakup of the smooth plane that had been their life together, the children had become, somehow, twelve, ten, and eight.

He had won a really spectacular fellowship at Columbia, three years being paid twice what he made at Cornell and no teaching, and a chance to work beside the man who was tops in his field. Peter asked Beatrice what she thought, but only formally. They both knew. They would be going to New York.

Nights in the house ten miles above Ithaca—it was summer and in her panic she could hear the crickets and, toward dawn, smell the freshness of the wet grass—she lay awake in terror of the packing job ahead of her. Everything, each thing she owned, would have to be wrapped and collected. She lived in dread of losing something, breaking something, for each carefully selected, carefully tended object that she owned was a proof of faith against the dark clutching power of the past. She typed on an index card a brief but wholly accurate description of the house, and the housing office presented her with a couple from Berlin—particle physicists, the both of them, and without children, she was grateful to hear. They seemed clean and thorough; they wanted to live in the country, they were the type who would know enough to act in time if a problem were occurring, who wouldn't let things get too far.

Peter and Beatrice were assured by everyone they talked to in New York that their apartment was a jewel. Sally Rodier, the wife of Peter's collaborator, who also helped Beatrice place the children in private schools, kept telling her how incredibly lucky they were, to have been given an apartment in one of the buildings on Riverside Drive. The view could be better, but they had a glimpse of the river. Really, they were almost disgustingly lucky, she said, laughing. Did they know what people would do to get what they had?

But Beatrice's heart sank at the grayness of the grout between the small octagonal bathroom floor tiles, the uneven job of polyurethaning on the living room floor, the small hole in the floor by the radiator base, the stiff door on one of the kitchen cabinets, the frosted glass on the window near the shower that she couldn't, whatever she did, make look clean.

For nearly a month she worked, making the small repairs herself, unheard-of behavior, Sally Rodier said, in a Columbia tenant. She poured a lake of bleach on the bathroom floor, left it for six hours, then, sopping it up, found she had created a field of dazzling whiteness. She made curtains; she scraped the edges of the window frames. Then she began to venture out. She had been so few places, had done so little, that the city streets, although they frightened her, began to seem a place of quite exciting possibilities. Because she did her errands, for the first time in her life, on foot, she could have human contact with no fear of revelation. She could be among her kind without fear every second that they would find out about her: where and what she'd come from, who she really was. Each day the super left mail on her threshold; they would exchange a pleasant word or two. He was a compact and competent man who had left his family in Peru. She could imagine that he and the Bangladeshi doormen, and the people on the streets, all possessed a dark and complicated past, things they'd prefer to have hidden as she did. In Buffalo, in Ithaca, people had seemed to be expressing everything they were. Even their reserves seemed legible and therefore relatively simple. But, riding on the bus and walking out on Broadway, she felt for the first time part of the web of concealment, of lives constructed like a house with rooms that gave access only to each other, rooms far from the initial entrance, with no source of natural light.

By Thanksgiving, she was able to tell Peter, who feared that she would suffer separation from her beloved house, that she was enjoying herself very much. The boys, whose lives, apart from their aspects of animal survival, never seemed to have much to do with her, were absorbed in the thick worlds of their schools— activities till five or six most nights, homework, and supper and more homework. Weekends, she could leave them to Peter, who was happy to take them to the park for football, or to the university pool, or the indoor track. She would often go to the Metropolitan Museum, to look at the collection of American furniture or, accompanied by a guide book, on an architectural tour.

One Thursday night, Peter was working in the library and the boys were playing basketball in the room the two younger ones shared, throwing a ball made of foam through the hoop Peter had nailed against the door. Beatrice was surprised to hear the bell ring; people rarely came without telephoning first. She opened the door to a stranger, but catching a glimpse of her neighbor across the hall, a history professor, opening her door, she didn't feel afraid.

The man at the doorway was unlike anyone she had spoken to in New York, anyone she'd spoken to since she'd left home. But in an instant she recognized him. She thought he was there to tell her the story of her life, and to tell Peter and everyone she knew. She'd never met him, as himself, before. But he could have lived in the house she'd been born in. He had an unrushed look, as if he had all the time in the world. He took a moment to meet her eyes, but when he did, finally, she understood the scope of everything he knew.

She kept the door mostly closed, leaving only enough space for her body. She would allow him to hurt her, if that was what he came for, but she wouldn't let him in the house.

"I'm your downstairs neighbor," he said.

She opened the door wider. He was wearing a greasy-looking ski jacket which had once been royal blue; a shiny layer of black grime covered the surface like soot on old snow. The laces on his black sneakers had no tips. His pants were olive green; his hands were in his pockets. It was impossible to guess how old he was. He was missing several top teeth, which made him look not young, but his hair fell over his eyes in a way that bestowed youth. She stepped back a pace further into the hall.

"What can I do for you?"

"You've got kids?"

For a moment, she thought he meant to take the children. She could hear them in the back of the apartment, running, laughing, innocent of what she was sure would befall them. A sense of heavy torpor took her up. She felt that whatever this man wanted, she would have to let him take. A half-enjoyable lassitude came over her. She knew she couldn't move.

He was waiting for her answer. "I have three boys," she said.

"Well, what you can do for me is to tell them to stop their racket. All day, all night, night and day, bouncing the ball. The plaster is coming down off the ceiling. It's hitting me in my bed. That's not too much to ask, is it? You can see that's not too much to ask."

"No, of course not. No," she said. "I'll see to it right away."

She closed the door very quickly. Walking to the back part of the apartment, she had to dig her nails into the palms of her hands so that she wouldn't scream the words to her children. "They didn't know, they didn't know," she kept saying to herself. It wasn't their fault. They weren't used to living in an apartment. It wasn't anybody's fault. But she was longing to scream at them, for having made this happen. For doing something so she would have to see that man, would have to think about him. An immense distaste for her children came over her. They seemed loud and gross and spoiled and careless. They knew nothing of the world. They were passing the ball back and forth to one another, their blond hair gleaming in the light that shone down from the fixture overhead.

She forced herself to speak calmly. "I'm afraid you can't play basketball here," she said. "The man downstairs complained."

"What'd you say to him?" asked Jeff, the oldest.

"I said I'd make you stop."

"What'd you say that for? We have just as much right as he does."

She looked at her son coldly. "I'm afraid you don't."

The three of them looked back at her, as if they'd never seen her.

"I'll make supper now," she said. "But I have a terrible head-ache. After I put dinner on the table, I'm going to lie down."

While she was cooking, the phone rang. It was her neighbor across the hall. "Terribly sorry to intrude," she said. "I hope I'm not being a busybody, but I couldn't help overhear the rather unpleasant exchange you had with our neighbor. I just thought you should understand a few things."

I understand everything, Beatrice wanted to say. There's nothing I don't understand.

"He's a pathetic case. Used to be a big shot in the chemistry department. Boy genius. Then he blew it. Just stopped going to classes, stopped showing up in the department. But some bigwigs in the administration were on his side, and he's been on disability and allowed to keep the apartment. We're all stuck with him. If he ever opens the door and you're near, you get a whiff of the place. Unbelievable. It's unbelievable how people live. What I'm trying to tell you is, don't let him get you bent out of shape. Occasionally he crawls out of his cave and growls something, but he's quite harmless."

"Thank you," said Beatrice. "Thank you for calling. Thank you very much."

She put down the phone, walked into her bedroom, turned out all the lights, and lay down on her bed.

Lying in the dark, she knew it was impossible that he was underneath her. If his room was below the children's, it was near the other side of the apartment, far from where she was.

But she imagined she could hear his breathing. It matched her own: in-out-in-out. Just like hers.

She breathed with him. In and out, and in and out. Frightened, afraid to leave the bed, she lay under a quilt she'd made herself. She forced herself to think of the silver scissors, her gold thimble, the spools and spools of pale thread. Tried and tried to call them back, a pastel shimmering cloud, a thickness glowing softly in this darkness. It would come, then fade, swallowed up in darkness. Soon the darkness was all there was. It was everything. It was everything she wanted and her only terror was that she would have to leave it and go back. Outside the closed door, she could hear the voices of her husband and her sons. She put her fingers in her ears so she couldn't hear them. She prayed, she didn't know to whom, to someone who inhabited the same darkness. This was the only thing about the one she prayed to that she knew. She prayed that her family would forget about her, leave her. She dreaded the door's cracking, the intrusion of the light. If she could just be here, in darkness, breathing in and out, with him as he breathed in and out. Then. Then she didn't know. But it would be something that she feared.

"How about you tone it down and let your mother sleep?"

She closed her eyes as tightly as a child in nightmare. Then she knew that she had been, in fact, asleep because when Peter came in, sank his weight onto the bed, she understood she had to start pretending to be sleeping.

After that night, she began staying in bed all day long. She had so rarely been sick, had met the occasional cold or bout of flu with so much stoicism that Peter couldn't help but believe her when she complained of a debilitating headache. And it would have been impossible for him to connect her behavior with the man downstairs. He hadn't even seen him. No one had seen him except her and the woman across the hall who told her what she didn't need to know, what she already knew, what she couldn't help knowing.

She wondered how long it would be before Peter suggested calling a doctor. That was what worried her as she lay in the darkness: what would happen, what would be the thing she wouldn't be able to resist, the thing that would force her to get up.

She cut herself off fully from the life of the family. She had no idea what kind of life was going on outside her door. Peter was coping very well, without a question or murmur of complaint. Cynically, she thought it was easier for him not to question: he might learn something he didn't want to know. He had joined up with her so they could create a world free from disturbance, from disturbances. Now the disturbance rumbled beneath them, and it only stood to reason that he wouldn't know of it and wouldn't want to know.

Each morning, she heard the door close as Peter left with the children for school. Then she got up, bathed, fixed herself a breakfast, and, exhausted, fell back into a heavy sleep. She would sleep through the afternoon. In the evening, Peter brought her supper on a tray. The weak light from the lamp on the bed table hurt her eyes; the taste and textures of the food hurt her palate, grown fragile from so much silence, so much sleep.

She didn't ask what the children were doing and they didn't come in to see her. Peter assumed she was in excruciating pain. She said nothing to give him that idea, and nothing to relieve him of it.

After her fourth day in the dark, she heard the doorbell ring. It was early evening, the beginning of December. Night had completely fallen and the radiators hissed and cooed. She tried not to hear what was going on outside, so at first she only heard isolated words that Peter was shouting. "Children." "Natural." "Ordinary." "Play." "Rights." "No right."

Alarm, a spot of electric blue spreading beneath one of her ribs, made her understand that Peter was shouting at the man downstairs. She jumped out of bed and stood at the door of the bedroom. She could see Peter's back, tensed as she had, in fourteen years of marriage, never seen it. His fists were clenched at his side.

"You come here, bothering my wife, disturbing my family. I don't know where the hell...what makes you think...but you've got the wrong number, mister. My sons are going to play ball occasionally at a reasonable hour. It's five-ten in the afternoon. Don't tell me you're trying to sleep."

"All right, buddy. All right. We'll just see about sleeping. Some night come midnight when everyone in your house is fast asleep, you want to hear about disturbing. Believe me, buddy, I know how to make a disturbance."

Peter shut the door in the man's face. He turned around, pale, his fists not yet unclenched.

"Why didn't you tell me about that guy?" he said, standing so close to her that his voice hurt her ears, which had heard very little in the last four days.

"I wasn't feeling well," she said.

He nodded. She knew he hadn't heard her.

"Better get back into bed."

The doorbell rang again. Peter ran to it, his fists clenched once again. But it wasn't the man downstairs, it was the woman across the hall. Beatrice could hear her telling Peter the same story she'd told her, but with more details. "The house is full of broken machines, he takes them apart for some experiment he says he's doing. He says he's going to be able to create enough energy to power the whole world. He brags that he can live on five dollars a week."

"Low overhead," said Peter, and the two of them laughed.

She was back in the darkness. Her heart was a swollen muscle; she spread her hands over her chest to slow it down. She heard Peter calling Al Rodier.

"Do you believe it . . . university building . . . speak to someone in real estate first thing . . . right to the top if necessary . . . will not put up with it . . . hard to evict, but not impossible. Despoiling the environment . . . polluting the air we breathe."

The word "pollution" spun in her brain like one of those headlines in old movies: one word finally comprehensible after the turning blur: Strike. War.

Pollution. It suggested a defilement so complete, so permanent, that nothing could reverse it. Clear streams turned black and tar-like, verdant forests transformed to soot-covered stumps, the air full of black flakes that settled on the skin and couldn't be washed off.

Was that what the man downstairs was doing? He was living the way he wanted to, perhaps the only way he could. Before this incident, he hadn't disturbed them. They were the first to disturb him. People had a right not to hear thumping over their heads. Supposing he was trying to read, listening to music, working out a scientific formula. Suppose, when the children were making that noise, he was on the phone making an important call, the call that could change his life.

It wasn't likely. What was more likely was that he was lying in the dark, as she was. But not as she was. He wasn't lying in an empty bed. He bedded down in garbage. And the sound of thumping over his head was the sound of all his fear: that he would be named the names that he knew fit him, but could bear if they weren't said. "Disreputable." "Illegitimate."

They would send him out into the world. If only he could be left alone. If only he could be left to himself. And her children with their loud feet, the shouts of their unknowingness told him what he most feared, what he was right to fear, but what he only wanted to forget. At any minute they would tell him he was nothing, he was worse than nothing. Everything was theirs and they could take it rightfully, at any moment. Not because they were unjust or cruel. They were not unjust. Justice was entirely on their side. He couldn't possibly, in justice, speak a word in his own defense. Stone-faced, empty-handed, he would have to follow them into the open air.

She heard Peter on the phone calling the people they knew in the building who'd invited them for coffee or for brunch. She kept hearing him say his name—Peter Talbot—and his department—Mathematics, and the number of their apartment—4A. He was urging them to band together in his living room, the next night, to come up with a plan of action before, he kept saying, over and over, "things get more out of hand. And when you think," he kept saying, "of the qualified people who'd give their eyeteeth for what he's got, what he's destroying for everyone who comes after him. I'll bet every one of you knows someone who deserves that apartment more than him."

She saw them filing into her house, their crisp short hair, their well-tended shoes, the smiles cutting across their faces like a rifle shot. They would march in, certain of their right to be there, their duty to keep order. Not questioning the essential rightness of clearing out the swamp, the place where disease bred, and necessarily, of course, removing the breeders and the spreaders who, if left to themselves, would contaminate the world.

And Beatrice knew that they were right, that was the terrible thing about them, their unquestionable rightness. Right to clear out, break in, burn, tear, demolish, so that the health of the world might be preserved.

She sank down deeper. She was there with those who wallowed, burrowed, hoarded, their weak eyes half-closed, their sour voices, not really sour but hopeless at the prospect of trying to raise some objection, of offering some resistance. They knew there could be no negotiation, since they had no rights. So their petition turned into a growl, a growl that only stiffened the righteousness of their purpose. "Leave me alone," is all the ones who hid were saying. They would have liked to beseech but they were afraid to. Also full of hate. "Leave me alone."

Of course they wouldn't be left alone. They couldn't be. Beatrice understood that.

The skin around her eyes felt flayed, her limbs were heavy, her spine too weak to hold her up. "Leave me alone." The sweetness of the warm darkness, like a poultice, was all that could protect her from the brutality of open air on her raw skin.

She and the man downstairs breathed. In and out. She heard their joined breath and, underneath that sound, the opening of doors, the rush of violent armies, of flame, of tidal wave, lightning cleaving a moss-covered tree in two. And then something else below that: "Cannot. Cannot. Leave me alone." Unheeded.

She turned the light on in the bedroom. She put on a pair of light blue sweatpants and a matching sweatshirt. On her feet she wore immaculate white socks and the white sneakers she'd varnished to brilliance with a product called Sneaker White she'd bought especially. She put on earrings, perfume, but no lipstick and no blush. She walked out of the apartment. She knew that Peter, in the back with the children, wouldn't hear the door close.

She walked down the dank, faintly ill-smelling stairs to the apartment situated exactly as hers was—3A—and rang the bell.

He opened the door a crack. The stench of rotting food and unwashed clothes ought to have made her sick, but she knew she was beyond that sort of thing.

She looked him in the eye. "I need to talk to you," she said.

He shrugged then smiled. Most of his top teeth were gone and the ones that were left were yellowed and streaked. He pushed the lock of his blondish hair that fell into his forehead back, away from his eyes. Then he took a comb out of his pocket and pulled it through his hair.

"Make yourself at home," he said, laughing morosely.

There was hardly a place to stand. The floor space was taken up by broken radios, blenders, ancient portable TVs revealing blown tubes, disconnected wires, a double-size mattress. Beside the mattress were paper plates with hardened sandwiches, glimpses of pink ham, tomatoes turned to felt between stone-colored slices of bread, magazines with wrinkled pages, unopened envelopes (yellow, white, mustard-colored), sloping hills of clean underwear mixed up with balled socks, and opened cans of Coke. There were no sheets on the mattress; sheets, she could tell, had been given up long ago. Loosely spread over the blue ticking was a pinkish blanket, its trim a trap, a bracelet for the foot to catch itself in during the uneasy night.

A few feet from the mattress was a Barcalounger whose upholstery must once have been mustard-colored. The headrest was a darker shade, almost brown; she understood that the discoloration was from the grease of his hair when he leaned back. She moved some copies of *Popular Mechanics* and some Styrofoam containers, hamburger-sized, to make room for herself to sit. She tried to imagine what she looked like, in her turquoise sweatsuit, sitting in this chair.

"I came to warn you," she said. "They're having a meeting. Right now in my apartment. They want to have you evicted."

He laughed, and she could see that his top teeth looked striated, lines of brownish yellow striping the enamel in a way she didn't remember seeing on anyone else.

"Relax," he said. "It'll never happen. They keep trying, but it'll never happen. This is New York. I'm a disabled person. I'm on disability. You understand what that means? Nobody like me gets evicted in New York. Don't worry about it. I'll be here forever."

She looked at her neighbor and gave him a smile so radiant that it seemed to partake of prayer. And then a torpor that was not somnolent, but full of joy, took hold of her. Her eyes were closing themselves with happiness. She needed rest. Why hadn't she ever known before that rest was the one thing she had always needed?

She saw her white bathroom floor, gleaming from the lake of bleach she had poured on it. Just thinking of it hurt her eyes.

Here, there was nothing that would hurt her. She wanted to tell him it was beautiful here, it was wonderful, it was just like home. But she was too tired to speak. And that was fine, she knew he understood. Here, where they both were, there was no need to say a word.

But he was saying something. She could hear it through her sleep, and she had to swim up to get it, like a fish surfacing for crumbs. She couldn't seem, quite, to open her eyes and she fell back down to the dark water. Then she felt him shaking her by the shoulders.

"What are you doing? What are you doing? You can't do that here."

She looked at his eyes. They weren't looking at her kindly. She had thought he would be kind. She blinked several times, then closed her eyes again. When she opened them, he was still standing above her, his hands on her shoulders, shaking them, his eyes unkind.

"You can't do that here. You can't just come down here and go to sleep like that. This is my place. Now get out."

He was telling her she had to leave. She supposed she understood that. She couldn't stay here if he didn't want her. She had thought he'd understand that what she needed was a place to rest, just that, she wouldn't be taking anything from him. But he was treating her like a thief. He was making her leave as if she were a criminal. There was no choice now but to leave, shamefully, like a criminal.

He closed the door behind her. Although her back was to the door, she felt he was closing it in her face and she felt the force of it exactly on her face as if his hand had struck it. She stood completely still, her back nearly touching the brown door.

She couldn't move. She couldn't move because she could think of no direction that seemed sensible. But the shame of his having thrown her out propelled her toward the stairs. She wondered if she could simply walk out of the building as she was. With no coat, no money, nothing to identify her. But she knew that wasn't possible. It was winter, and it was New York.

She walked up the stairs. She stood on the straw mat in front of her own door. She'd have to ring the bell; she hadn't brought her keys. Peter would wonder where she had gone. She didn't know what she'd tell him. There was nothing to say.

She didn't know what would happen now. She knew only that she must ring the bell and see her husband's face and then walk into the apartment. It was the place she lived and she had nowhere else to go.

Chiaroscuro

When, how far back? When I played
in a formal park, Grandmother watching from
a bench, the chalky whiteness of
the gravel glistening in the sun
wiping away all that passed before me,
indistinct summonings in the blaze,
by contrast the deep shade from trees so dark
I ran out from there fast as I could.
Or when, much older though still
in knee socks and short pants,
one afternoon near an outdoor swimming pool
I had gazed in amazement at
an older youth under a shower head,
water pouring as long as he pulled
the chain attached to it
and I stood at a distance
barefoot on the grass. On the way home
crossing the bridge I leaned
over the railing and for a long time
looked below at the barges passing under it.
What other than their cargo did
they bring? I stared at
the hull, black, smeared and discolored
slowly moving by. From where did
they come and where will they unload?
When the maid had let me in she said
my friend whom she referred to as
"your god" had telephoned. From my room
I caught, heart pounding, framed in
the window across, a glimpse of
a fully naked figure smooth and white
as statuary that had stepped quickly back

into the darkness letting the drapery
fall into place. Mirage or a true vision
from out of a past not yet mine,
the body shining forth aloof, sublime?
What was it in what lay hidden
that even then had hinted at
spectacular sounds and sights
beyond such I would hear and face,
would pursue and one day embrace?
Other than songs of yearning I had heard
at late sunset as the Ferris wheel barely turned
and two figures had followed a third into
the dark of trees. Steadily, steadily,
the unheard drone no matter what
the melody, the distant glow even when
the dimness in the sky was gone and
one blackbird shrieked among the trees.

Or, years later, a scene that though in
a dream is vivid still: I come in
upon a square, in a house opposite
a single window is lit, dark the square,
the sky alone is glittering;
from all sides, from out of a deep
distance, there is a music for which
there is no visible source. I near
the house, look in the window, stare at
two naked figures on a bed, bodies
so perfect only inspired masters
could have conceived of them, and
from there saw first expressed
a love that too desired to be real,
no human claim would keep,
no pleading retain. And later again
when having one day in class
on turning around looked straight into
a fellow student's eyes as though
finding there the self revealed

and knew that what had amazed me then
would one day have to be my own,
what but apparitions followed
in the years ahead when the figure
having stepped forth from out of the dark,
looked at in daylight would always fade back—
for it will not be trapped
what had infused itself in eyes
as pools in limbs as grace,
each an apparition of the elusive self,
interplays of shade or, dark at
the edges, imperceptible light; intrusions
as when a legendary bird
on having achieved a god's desire, rose up
and disappeared back into the clouds.

Intrigued early on
by shapes and scenes against
a background dim or luminous,
a master's strokes on canvas—
and we may or may not have held
incarnate in the best of terms
what eludes and we will not possess—
we are moved in the end not so much
by what we have come upon as by
the feeling we are left with when
whatever provoked it is gone.

Despite dissolutions of
astounding figurations close at hand,
a foggy nothingness as that in dreams,
beyond the line where the sea moves in,
where oleanders bloom
and a steep slope dense with acacias
ascends into mountains that ring a port,
beyond its shady ridges, the land's blue
invisibleness begins and ends.

Fanny Burney; Or, The Anatomy Theater

Chrome made echoes of the room. He closed the door.
It closed again, in accidental mirrors, warping
    On the cylinders for cotton,
Gauze, and was comical, not comical.

He closed the door, and let me watch him with his hands.
    I watched him wash his impressive hands
In his office. Did I need a nurse with me?

And then he drew what he learned of my anatomy.
    Water poured; I heard it end.
Swift— He made a pantomime above the breast
And told me to undress. And three times he predicted

    My abiding gratitude.
That was only part of what Fanny Burney knew;
The pantomime above her breast with his knife.

    "He never pats *my* arm,"
My mother said, and she dispensed with her jeopardy
With etiquette, as though it could be watered down;
    It could be evenings, rounded

With amateur theatricals: Fanny Burney's
Light impromptu pirouettes for the surgeon,
    Unwanted suitor, a surrogate mother.

What kind of praise for the mother of mastectomies?
In the years when history was taken for
    A comedy, a critic snorted,
"She wept, a talent much admired in her century."

Then he explained, as to a child, surgery
 Was like the waltz, not shocking for long,
And not the grand adventure. It was not.

She heard, boiling on the other side of the water,
 "Who will hold the breast for me?"
And seven doctors held her, though she stammered, "Please,
Shall I help? Shall I hold it for you, sir?"

 When will he ask how I am?
His interest would have made the scene more human.
I told him again my gratitude, but—"You should be glad.

 "Years ago, with this, you'd be dead."
But she went on; she bought a cottage; had evenings
Of educational amusements, "Pan piping
 For the rooster automata."

I was slow, beyond a vulnerability
Designed to flatter him. And slow to leave, smiling
 Over him and into his eyes,

As examples of gladness. I admire the works beholden
To aggression: Surgery, poetry.
 And with a comic twist of fate,
I too will buy a cottage; have evenings and play.

The Other Girls in Lettuce

These are the reminiscent lettuces,
And girls with pockets full of teeth
Will disappear in them, in fields of watered lettuce.
They sing when no one watches them in lettuce.
"Love what no one else would love. No one
Else would do it." They dot the far rows of lettuce,
Scavengers, enamored of the lettuces:
Their rapid filling out in light; and loud
When broken, loved and broken. The loudest
Mastication! Jaws ache in opened lettuce,
As they pick the blushing heads and hide.
If girls are eating, they will have to hide.

They mob the hazel shadows and they hide,
Stuffing their mouths with early lettuces,
With pampered butterheads; radicchios; they hide
With escarole, bending smaller; hide.
They had to do it—grab her with their teeth
And tear the subcutaneous fat. Oh make them hide!
What was chosen, what was trash, and what will hide?
Distant mother, distant girls. No one
Wants to hear what they did. No one
Hears them lick pretty lips in hiding,
Because the pinkest girls are not allowed
To hunger, touching thighs to come. Not allowed.

No blood on thighs or thoughts allowed
Except in hiding. "Alleluia!" In hiding,
This aberrance—this ravaging allowed.
She tasted like an afterlife allowed.
Then palate cleansers: Vinegar on lettuces,
Vinegar on massive greens allowed.
Did they do it? Was her death allowed?
No one knew the girls who did it with their teeth,

Who held her down; cut, tearing open; teeth
Devoured her. Alleged longing can be loud
And trembling; a pain known,
In dreams, as what they wanted to forget; no—

They wanted that preemptive banquet, but no
Tattletales of loneliness allowed.
They murmur, breathy moppet voices: "No one
Else would chew until it bleeds"; and know
They did it; fear it; diet; carry the fear in hiding:
Fury squeezed to a squeaking no one knows.
Call it giggling, and no one knows.
The future can be eaten like the past, with lettuce
And a cartoon vinaigrette, a tiny tune for lettuce.
No one questioned waking girls. No one
Claimed her body. No identifying teeth.
Shhh: Their pockets kept her gathered teeth

A secret. There, they pet her teeth,
Holding them as baby cups for tears. They know
Their curves, charms, and lick her teeth,
Tasting such possession. She left them all her teeth.
And days of anorexic industry, singing, loud,
"Grinding love to lettuce with our teeth!"
A half-remembered whistle couples air and teeth.
Never there; they play at blaming her and hide.
And love to think of her, hiding
In their love. They kiss the bracelets of her teeth:
The ivory on ivory, a luscious
Subterfuge; imagined matricide and lettuces.

Daughters want to stay with their lettuces
And work, the awful work they do in hiding,
Hushing appetites. They whisper, clenching teeth,
"Love her more than anyone." Anyone knows
Words are nipples still allowed.

JOHN R. KEENE

My Son, My Heart, My Life

S *andalwood,* Jaime whispers to himself, recalling the vendor
who had sold Tony and him the three little vials of this scented
oil and the five foil packets of incense. He had a makeshift stall
outside the bus terminal in Dudley Square. Wearing an embroi-
dered red and black tarboosh and an immaculately white T-shirt,
on which had been silk-screened in exquisite calligraphics the
simple phrase, "Life is the finest art," he was probably in his early
twenties—and *handsome,* Jaime thought now—though hard living had so weathered his face and hands, his gestures, that he
looked much older. Beside Tony, however, the vendor had
appeared almost a boy. His thin, dark fingertips, sallowed by the
oils, the incense, cigarettes, perhaps even the plate of curried goat
that sat at the edge of the display table, fanned slowly over the
array of offerings, patchouli, lavender, musk, Rose of Sharon,
anise, something called "Love," something else called "Power,"
which Jaime had not noticed before. Which one *you* like? *Sandalwood,* Tony had snapped out without deliberation: It was the only
scent he had ever worn.

—What*ever* you do, baby, don't forget your algebra notebook!
Jaime's mother's call rings from the kitchen, where she is preparing breakfast for his two younger sisters, Tatiana and Tasha. Having awoken early as always with his older sister, Teresita, Jaime has
already wolfed down a banana and a piece of white bread with
strawberry jelly for breakfast, before his mother and the girls rise,
to stay out of their way. Sometimes he will drink a cup of coffee
and chat with Teresita—whose position at the nearby springs
manufacturing plant occasions *her* early mornings—but not this
morning. He has spent the entire time since he woke, ate, and
showered in reading over his poem—*his poem!*—which his
teacher and classmates, everyone, including perhaps even his
mother, will all be talking about for weeks to come, and checking
his equations. After proofing his Spanish against the dictionary,

he struggled over a seemingly unsolvable *"xy,"* and came up with
the only answer that allowed the equation to work: This, he tells
himself, calls for a celebration, a *game.*

—*Sí,* Mami, I promised you I wasn't gonna forget it again. That
stupid notebook, Jaime grumbles, why can't he forget it altogether! He sits up on his bed, which he has just prepared to his mother's former specifications (since Tony's death, she no longer has to
scold him every morning, he now makes it instinctively), and
opens the palm-size, amber-colored vial, one of the few personal
effects of Tony's that neither his mother nor Tony's girlfriend had
hoarded as her own. As he had observed Tony do every morning
for the last few years, he places his index finger over the opening,
upends it, then daubs the sweet, masculine fragrance under both
ears; again, then lightly across his collarbone; one last time, a
straight line from the point where his Adam's apple has begun to
appear to the soft point of his chin.

This fragrance, Jaime realizes, almost smiling now, almost tearing as it takes root and blossoms in the loam of his consciousness,
still lingers upon the surface of everything in the apartment: this
matted wool comforter on which he sits; on the top and corners
of the particleboard dresser that he and Tony had shared; upon
even the mildewed plastic anti-slip stars plastering the bottom of
the bathtub in which they had stood huddled together when they
were younger, all redolent as though permanently coated. Today,
for good luck's sake, it will trail him as well, throughout the
morning, on the way to school, as he stands before his class and
reads his poem.

Done, he shakes his head as Tony would, wipes his eyes—no
one had seen him cry at or after the funeral and will not now—
then hides the vial under the stack of underpants in the top drawer of the dresser that has become his alone. As he stands before
the open drawer—how they had fought over where their clothes
would go! How he, Jaime, had *always* lost and wished that he
could claim the entire thing as his own!—he feels like a blackboard from which everything has been erased, on which anything
can be written. Tony. Alone, he drops onto the bed, tries to think
of the day before him, the bus ride, school…his poem. His
poem, which Tony would have read with approval, maybe even

awe, as he had done with the other poems, the drawings, the stories Jaime would write, sometimes off the top of his head....

Silent now, he can hear beneath the floorboards his uncle, Narciso, rearranging the merchandise on the shelves of the bodega he and his aunt Marisol own and operate. Above him, their apartment slumbers. Jaime is glad to have been occupied and to not have had to help out this morning. Often his mother will send him downstairs after she has awakened the girls and begun to get them ready and before his bus arrives, to seek something to do, to help his uncle and aunt out, as if she owes them something for living here, especially since his father left, as if his sacrifice is her part of the bargain. Sometimes he aids in moving pieces of meat around the cold-locker and shelving newly arrived canned and boxed goods when his uncle asks him to. Undoubtedly there will be some bubble-gum box to be refilled, some soup cans to be shifted around or transformed into a stable pyramid, some moldy bread to be turned over so that the nearby loaves will mask it. This morning, however, her mind has latched completely on to that notebook.

Outside this room, music, laughter, the cacophony of glass against metal, voices, the television against the hour's stillness.

Tony, Jaime reminds himself, had never helped out in the store. He had gone simply from mornings and afternoons before the television and Nintendo games to the streets and a crew of similarly minded boys and couriering, which meant that Uncle Narciso and Aunt Marisol never wanted him around; his presence, at least in their eyes, and that of his boys, his *chicos,* usually spelt trouble. It was an out to which Jaime had no recourse: *Send Jaime down to help me out,* Uncle Narciso was always saying, *so I can make a man out of him, keep him out of trouble.* Jaime's mother only too eagerly assented.

Hoisting his backpack onto the bed, Jaime pulls out his Spanish poem to read once more, which jogs his memory: they had had to wait until nearly the end of the school to write poems, and why? Because of the "turdles," as he and Vinh, his classmate and best and only friend, have often laughed to themselves at lunch, though neither would dare call the mass of their classmates, even the girls, this nickname face-to-face. Despite the fact that they have occasionally had to write a paragraph, or even a short essay, they are mainly doing multiple-choice quizzes, nothing more advanced, more creative, even though this class is supposedly accelerated. As usual Mrs. Donovan has given them nine regular words and a bonus word, and this time, unlike before, she has allowed them to create *a poem* of at least one hundred words from these. *Too simple,* Vinh had cracked under his breath, against the general groans of the class; Jaime had nodded, though he disagreed. As the lines now sing inside his head, he is sure this poem will merit an A, as will Vinh's, which he has not yet seen. Most of the other kids, even those whose first language is Spanish, will end up with B's or C's, whether they hand in homework or not, since Mrs. Donovan is unwilling to embarrass anyone, even the most "slow-dropping" of the turdles, with anything lower. They had to wait almost the entire year, Jaime sighs, but now he will show them.

The words read, in this order: *hijo* (son), *parar* (to stop), *pedir* (to ask for), *cada* (each), *corazón* (heart), *broma* (joke), *hallar* (to come across), *sangre* (blood), *anochecer* (nightfall), and the bonus word *fugaz* (brief).

Such words! Vinh had said after fourth period that Mrs. Donovan had torn up a Spanish dictionary and picked the entries one by one out of a hat, but Jaime is convinced that she pulls some of them out of whatever she has been reading at home, some novel, some book of poetry, because there are always strange or unusual words, like *fugaz,* that are nowhere to be found in their Spanish book. He has never heard anyone, not his mother, nor Uncle Narciso nor Aunt Marisol, nor any of the Spanish speakers in the neighborhood or at church, nor even his grandmother, uncles, aunts, or cousins in Puerto Rico, ever use this bonus word *fugaz* even once in conversation—he and his sisters speak only English regularly, as did Tony—which for him is the giveaway. *This* word, he thinks, she has selected just for me.

As a result, he wrote (with the translation beneath it):

> *Cada día al anochecer*
> *voy esa cama y pienso*
> *sobre mi hermano muerto,*
> *Antonio José Barrett.*

Fue mi hermano solo
y tuvo quince años y medio.
Yo halle la sangre y su cuerpo
que estaba acostado
sobre la acera como un G.I. Joe.
Durante el funeral mi Mami preguntó
al Dios, "¿Por qué, God, por qué
mi hijo, mi corazón, mi vida, mi Tony
por qué my baby ahora?" Mi tío
Narciso dijo toda la iglesia,
"¡O Dios, mi amigos, quando la muerte
va parar?" Nadie le respondió.
Desde entonce hay una cosa que yo sé:
en mi barrio vivir es muy fugaz
y el futuro estará una broma grande.

Every day at nighttime
I see that bed and I think
about my dead brother,
Antonio José Barrett.
He was my only brother
and was fifteen and a half years old.
I found the blood and his body
lying on the sidewalk like a G.I. Joe.
During the funeral my mother asked
God, "How come, God, how come
my son, my heart, my life, my Tony
why my baby now?" My uncle
Narciso said to the whole church,
"Oh God, my friends, when
is the dying going to end?"
No one answered him.
Since then there is one thing I know:
in my neighborhood living is too brief
and the future is a great big joke.

One hundred and eleven words he counts, and he has used the past tense correctly every time; he has verified this twice this morning against his Spanish book. No misspellings that he can spot, and even some words they have not yet learned, but which he has gathered from regular conversations or his own reading:

Mrs. Donovan will *have to* give him an A! When he recites it, she will comment on the rhymes in Spanish, on the flow, on the *feeling:* in her eyes there is nothing *he can do wrong.*

What else is there for today? For social studies he has his notes for his presentation on a country in West Africa. He has elected to report on Senegal, where he imagines his father's (and mother's, maybe) ancestors came from, instead of Cape Verde, his other option. Jaime shuffles his note cards in order: there are seven. He makes sure they are all there, then stores them in his backpack on top of his Spanish notebook. He has no homework (when do they ever have homework?) for any of his other classes, except algebra. He glances again at the figures cleanly printed in that notebook and on the loose-leaf, and on which he spent two hours last night, and at least one this morning.

His sisters are clamoring in the kitchen, he can hear; his mother never tells them to shut up anymore, or even slaps Tasha when she talks back as she had always done before. Jaime never talked back in the first place, though she would still sometimes slap him for whatever reason (because he would not clean his room, because he sulked all through dinner, because he was switching and batting his eyes, because he reminded her too much of *that black man who had left her*) but now she is always asking him what he is doing before she gets home, how he is progressing in school, what he is *feeling. My son.* He always lies and tells her nothing beyond the barest outline of what happens to him each day, because he is convinced she would not understand anyway, or care; she has never understood a thing about him before in the previous thirteen and a half years of his life, nor cared, and she understood even less about Tony, whose name was always on her lips, though no longer. *Tony. My heart.* Nor about any of his sisters, except Tatiana, the *true* baby, who seems to gain her care and concern, though how long will *this* last, Jaime wonders, how long? *My life.*

Why is it so quiet downstairs? He descends the stairwell quietly and crosses the narrow hallway, through the double-hinged door, into the store. Quiet, empty. His uncle Narciso has obviously gone into the storeroom down in the cellar, or perhaps out into the small cold-locker in back, and Aunt Marisol has not yet come down. The shade on the front door is still drawn, and the triple-bolts have not been unlocked, nor the gratings raised and furled.

Jaime leans back against the wall of candy racks behind the cash register and brushes curly, raven bangs back from his forehead. In the mirror of Plexiglas surrounding the register area before him, he chances upon his reflection: the spit and image of his father—the eyes two new black backgammon chits; the nose the face's anchor, an inverted mahogany cross; the lips as pale and swollen as two undercooked link sausages—whose actual face he has not seen in two years, he finds himself *almost* handsome, though not like Tony, who more resembled their mother, and was thin, lean, wiry. He, Jaime, is still too plump, *"muy gordo."* Though no one calls him "Porcelito" anymore, since he has lost some weight over the last few months, his first cousin Niño, who had been a year ahead of him at school until he flunked out and was placed in Catholic school, has not stopped calling him "Gordon" every chance he can. At least he no longer has to hear that nickname at school, or Niño's other gem, "Chunky and Chinky," for when he and Vinh were together. Being *"gordo,"* however, no one has ever expected him to be cool or popular or have a girl-friend or have *juice.* Those expectations fell upon Tony, who satis-fied them amply, which allowed Jaime thus to be the inverse, his reverse: the "smart," "quiet," "artistic" one, the little chub who spends all his hours in his room, drawing, reading, writing, devis-ing imaginary scenarios and games by and for himself. . . .

Since Tony's death, however, not even Niño or his mother calls him those *other* names, those names that had lacerated Jaime in their truth and viciousness, that had left him in tears when not driving him to fights he could not win, though no one, not even his mother, had ever dared utter them in Tony's presence. That Tony would never tolerate, Jaime remembers, nor had he ever called Jaime those names, not even while playing, though he must have known. . . . Now, since Tony failed to father a little boy, he, Jaime, has become his mother's *only* son, the only *man* in her life . . . the thought sometimes makes him shudder, as now.

Mi hijo, mi corazón, mi vida.

Still by himself, he empties into his mouth an already-opened box of Lemon-Heads which was sitting under the register and probably belonged to Aunt Marisol, who is always munching on something sweet. At his feet he notices about six chewing-gum wrappers, which means that Aunt Marisol, or Lisa, a woman neighbor who fills in at night, worked the closing shift: Uncle Narciso would never tolerate trash lying anywhere on this floor, so he has not yet been back behind here. Jaime gathers them up and, as he is tossing them in the wastebasket, notices the Browning Hi-Power 9mm semiautomatic, clipless, poking out from the lower shelf. Who left this thing out? Catching no light the barrel does not flash as it normally would; Jaime's thoughts recoil from the cold metal. He has held this handgun before, and had held Tony's many times; with his toe he pushes it back onto the shelf so that it is no longer visible.

Before his uncle returns, he pulls the shade to peep out the front door. A small throng of people is collecting at the bus stop several feet down from the front of the store. This group of about seven people, all of them neighbors, mostly work downtown or in Cambridge, and there is a woman Jaime recognizes as one of the teacher's aides in the special education program now housed at the back of his school. Hardly anyone is milling around, as usual, so frozen are they to their spots, even at this time of year. Within seconds the bus, already half-full, screeches up. These commuters, as is customary, are pushing and shoving each other out of the way to board. Jaime's mother always says that the Orientals push hardest because they have to claim seats first or they will never be able to muscle their way into one, that Portuguese will give up their seats if you look tired enough because they are a sad people, that the Irish usually smell like whiskey or beer so you will want to give them your seat, that the West Indians do not care how tired you look if you do not look West Indian, and that black men never give up their seats for an older woman, unless it's their mother. But Jaime knows these kernels of maternal wisdom do not hold; he was once knocked out of his seat by another Puerto Rican, and Tony always gave up his seat for an older or pregnant woman, if she was black or Puerto Rican or Cape Verdean. Truth is, everyone, as Jaime knows, can be rude, mercenary, self-interested.

—¿Ai, Negrito, qué tal? Jaime feels the thick, spatulate fingers

softly digging into his shoulders, the protuberant stomach pressing against his slope of his shoulder blades. It is his uncle Narciso.
He tenses. His uncle's breath, warm and somewhat stale, wets the
hairs on the back of his neck, as his hand slips like a scarf around
Jaime's neck bone.

—*Nada, Tío.* Jaime turns around to face his uncle's sloe eyes, a
virtual mirror image of his mother, in male form. Of medium
height—Jaime has never been able to guess heights on sight, but
Narciso is taller than Tony, who was five-eight—and, like his
mother, slender, except for the belly, Jaime comes nearly to his
uncle's forehead. He backs away, to prevent his uncle's mustache
from scouring *his* forehead like a small hairbrush.

—You didn't come down this morning. *Tío* was waiting on
you. His uncle grins, exposing a row of teeth like kernels of Indian corn.

—I was working on my algebra. I'm *failing,* you know. Jaime
stops against the counter. I told you that, *Tío.* He knows his uncle
is not listening, as usual.

—*Tío* was *waiting* on you. I had a lot for you to do this morning, didn't your mother let you know? He approaches Jaime, both
his hands squirming beneath his bloody apron like two small,
trapped birds.

—I was just checking to make sure the bus was on schedule.
Jaime rolls his eyes, darting out of his uncle's path, towards an
aisle. I'm gonna be late if I don't hurry up, *Tío.*

—You don't got any time left to help *Tío* this morning! I was
waiting on you. Jaime cants his head around the corner to read the
clock: he has only about fifteen or twenty minutes before his bus
arrives. His uncle sweeps a lock off Jaime's forehead, reaches
down, and tightly embraces him. Like always, he is mouthing
something onto Jaime's earlobe, his neck, but Jaime has long since
stopped paying any attention; he just goes slack and waits for his
uncle to let go. In the back of the room, beyond the door to both
the apartments and the cold-locker, he can now hear someone,
probably his aunt Marisol, scuffling towards the storeroom in the
cellar. Abruptly his uncle releases him, picks up the cash box at his
feet, and slips behind the door that forms a clear, though somewhat rickety, protective partition around the register.

—I'll help out tomorrow morning, *Tío*, I promise, Jaime yells out, before bounding out of the store and upstairs so as not to be late. When he reaches the top of the stairs, he hears his mother saying:

—And I told Mr. Morris to call me if you was skipping class or not doing you homework, Jaime, because I don't want you failing math again. Had she heard him come upstairs or had she just automatically launched into this? he asks himself. His mother, splendid in her nurse's aide's whites, emerges from her bedroom, and now stands before him in the narrow strait of hallway between the rooms. She is frowning, blankly.

—Did you *hear* me?

—Yeah, Mami, I heard you. I'm not gonna skip algebra any more, and I *did* my homework, just like Mr. Morris wants. Do you want to *see* it? Do you want to see my *poem*? As though by default she shakes her head no; she seldom looks at any of his homework, though she will sometimes check to make sure that he has at least packed the notebook in with the rest of his school materials, and she never looks at his other things, his other notebooks, full of his writings and drawings, which he now keeps hidden behind his bed in a small bag that had belonged to Tony. Most of these he has shown to no one except Vinh, who draws pictures of his own, keeps similar notebooks. Vinh's consist mostly of action figures like the X-Men or the Fantastic Four, which he copies from the comic books he collects (Jaime collected them, too, at one point but stopped when his mother got laid off the last time), but he always changes all the eyes and hair so that they become Vietnamese and usually much more muscular than they appeared originally. Jaime's, all drawn from his storehouse of memories and fantasy, usually consist of people he has seen on the bus or on the street or in the bodega, or at Downtown Crossing or in Central Square when he slips there on Saturdays or sometimes after school, and occasionally he even draws pictures of Tony, and rarely his father, though never other members of his family. Other renderings, completely from his imagination and of a different, vivid, and more explicit nature, he reveals to no one. So much no one knows about him, he realizes, now that Tony is gone.

As they stand there wordlessly, Jaime places one hand on his hip and licks the palm of his free hand, flips back his bangs coquet-tishly, bats his eyes: this once provoked a reproach from his moth-er, but no longer. She stands before him, saying nothing, bemused as if she were looking upon someone she had never seen before in life, when his youngest sister, Tatiana, just barely five, materializes, her jumper misbuttoned and her socks mismatched, her ponytails uncoiling from beneath her barrettes. She drops in loud sobs to the floor at his mother's feet. Jaime flees into his bedroom.

A glance at the Teenage Mutant Ninja Turtle clock—had he really been *so* into them?—alerts him that he has only about five minutes to spare. He checks his backpack to ensure everything is there, including that stupid algebra notebook. He even makes sure that he has the loose-leaf of arithmetic work tucked into the front inside cover of the notebook; Mr. Morris likes to receive the homework this way, so that he can verify the answers in the note-book by the preparatory work on the loose-leaf. Only for such a white turdle, Jaime notes, does everything have to be so compli-cated. On top of this, Mr. Morris is always pushing Jaime to do better, cornering him after class, stopping him in the hallways, calling his mother *at home!—he could easily be an A student, Ms. Barrett*—but all those variables and commutative laws tend to drive Jaime to distraction; he likes Spanish and Language Arts and social studies much better, since they afford him the freedom to order things—words, worlds, his life—to his satisfaction. Still, he has to admit that there is no reason he should *fail* algebra, because if he does, it will probably spell the death of his chances of getting into the Latin Academy, where he, with Vinh, has vowed to be, come ninth grade.

Below the clock's green-diode glimmer, Jaime gathers up the change off the small desk he had shared with Tony, and funnels it into his pockets. Maybe he will buy a pack of doughnuts from Uncle Narciso to eat on the way, or maybe he will save the coins for a tonic after school. *Tony.* It is so quiet these mornings, and evenings, too, now that Tony is no longer around, and yet Jaime no longer has to keep quiet when he wakes for fear of awaking Tony, who would be lightly snoring by now after having come in just around dawn from a long night out, probably dealing. This last year and a half Jaime would occasionally find a few dollar bills, mostly ones but occasionally a five or ten, lying in his house shoes when, still half-asleep, he climbed out of bed to go to the bath-room in the morning, and he did not even have to look across the room to realize these signified Tony was home and installed under the covers. Jaime had been saving these small gifts, which totaled about fifty-six dollars after a few withdrawals, and now keeps them tied up in a sock in the back of his drawer, for a future emer-gency. He has told no one about this, not even Vinh.

As though it were a talisman, he fingers his sock-bank, re-stashing it carefully, then slips on a green, plastic wristband that he had won at the West Indian Festival last summer, before zip-ping up his backpack and heading downstairs.

His mother had said nothing about his yellow T-shirt, his baggy red shorts, or his matching red hightop sneakers when she saw him earlier. Teresita would surely say he looked like a clown, but she has left for work already. No one would even notice the wristband, he bets, or what the colors together represent. His keys: he pats the three of them, which hang from an extra-long shoelace beneath his shirt down into his briefs.

—Mami, I'm going. Where is she?

—Jaime? In the kitchen. He pokes his head in the doorway.

—You be good and be careful, okay?

—I will. She has Tasha in one hand and Tatiana in the other. The two girls are dressed like twins, even though Tasha is three years older. His mother is obviously on her way out as well.

—Jaime, you got your algebra notebook? He nods yes, tapping his backpack where he thinks it is tucked away—*because I just want you to do well, to not end up like your brother, to get out of all of this*—then gives her a quick kiss on the cheek.

As he runs down the stairs, he can hear the *I love you* trailing his steps.

Through the bodega, where his aunt Marisol is now planted behind the register, chewing on a stick of gum, past his uncle Narciso, who is lifting the last of the outside grates and larks out a goodbye in Spanish and English, onto the already hot, uneven, tar-gummed pavement: the bus has not yet arrived. Jaime crosses the street to his bus stop.

Only one other person is waiting for this bus: a young man,

Corey Fuentes, who had dated Jaime's sister Teresita. As Jaime looks up and smiles, Corey sneers in reply, then lights up his Newport. Corey is out of work, has been for about a year, Jaime has heard, but this morning he is wearing alligator loafers, nice pressed gray slacks, an ironed white shirt, and holds what appears to be a brand-new clip-on tie in his free hand, which leads Jaime to suppose that he is going in for a job interview (very unlikely), traveling somewhere to meet his parole officer or some new criminal associate (more likely but still unlikely), or heading downtown to make a court date (most likely). Jaime does not dare inquire.

The spring heat has not yet fired the streets, and a breeze, almost gauzy in texture, carries pieces of trash and some seedlings towards the horizon. The other bodega, owned by the Cape Verdeans, stands behind and cater-corner from them, somewhat dilapidated on the outside, with its warped grates, yellowed newspapered curtains, and its faded beer signs, unopened. To their right across the street in the distance, down near the wrought-iron fence that garters the Social Services building, a corpulent straw-haired white man, whom Jaime recognizes as Father Peter O'Hanlon, is chatting with a woman employee, unknown. So what if Fr. Pete was removed as assistant pastor of St. Stephen Protomartyr's for spending so much time with the gangs? Tony, Jaime remembers him saying, is not a lost cause. He will surely be in the bodega gossiping with Aunt Marisol and sipping a Coke, laced with rum, in about twenty minutes.

—Where *is* that fucking bus? Corey hisses, checking his wrist graced not by a watch, but by an ornate gold bracelet.

He leans backbreakingly against the bus-stop sign pole. He is staring off into the distance, envisioning what? Jaime wonders. What sort of plea bargain his attorney will arrange? Whether his new girlfriend will show up to escort him back home, on his own recognizance? What the penalty will be for "uttering checks and credit cards" for the third time within one calendar year? Jaime is familiar with quite a few of the court careers of other people, such as Tony, and Teresita's current boyfriend, Eric, and her ex-boyfriend Andray, so that it is not too difficult for him to figure out what this "small-time booster," as Tony had labeled him, might be facing.

As he ponders Corey's fate, his eyes trace an invisible line from the slicked, raven crown of hair to the full, pink lips to the satiny brown neck bone, which a white undershirt almost completely conceals from view. He has dreamt about Corey before. Jaime's eyes linger on that downward slope and the cloven pectorals below, imagining them supple beneath his grasping fingers like the earth beneath the saplings that his Earth Science class spent all last month planting. Corey's skinny arms pale in comparison to the knottier arms and the ample chest of the guy who sometimes drives Jaime's bus route—Jerome—whose name he has inscribed on the inside back cover of the notebook he remembered to bring with him today. For a while Jaime feared his mother might see this name and interrogate him about it, but then he realized she would not touch anything of his, save perhaps that algebra notebook, under any circumstances, unless *he* were dead.

Turning and catching Jaime in his spell of appreciation, Corey glowers, murmuring, —You li'l *freak*! As Jaime looks away, unembarrassed, Fr. Pete lumbers his way up the street.

Another breeze is bearing up a fresh offering of debris as their bus scuds up to the curb. Corey boards first, tamping out his cigarette and tossing it over his shoulder so that it bounces off Jaime's arm. Jaime says nothing, and hops aboard after him, perfunctorily flashing his pass as he moves into the aisle. The bus is mostly vacant, but before he can grab a seat, the bus driver has pulled sharply away into the street, stomping down on the accelerator, thus hurtling Jaime headfirst towards the back. Obviously, this bus driver is *not* Jerome, who has a velvet touch on the pedal—Jaime visually verifies this: No! Oh, well—but instead Randall, who from time to time works this morning route but more often drives the Columbia Road evening route, which Jaime has taken on those occasions when he had to drop off something at his sister Tita's job.

For a moment he debates whether he should sit up near Randall, whom he has never really paid much attention to, or sit in the back of the bus and write in his notebook: *¿Qué va hacer?* He decides to perch himself on the last forward-facing seat on the right side of the bus, near no one; Corey is sitting near most of the other passengers in the forward-facing seats near the front, an unlit cigarette poling from his lips. Jaime thinks about reading his poem, how his classmates will all stare in amazement, how Mrs. Donovan will nod her head appreciatively with theirs, how afterwards she will tell him that this is proof of what she knows he can do. He will show her his other poems, some of his drawings soon, she will write a recommendation for him, he will get into Boston Latin, he will do so well that he confirms Tony's grandest predictions. He tries not to think about algebra at all.

Randall's driving this morning is certainly a lot more jerky than Jerome's. Extracting his writing notebook and a pencil, he sketches Randall's face, and then Jerome's face and torso, which he can summon from memory as sharply as if he were staring right at them, before writing beneath both pictures: "AM: RANDALL—Almost turdle of the bus drivers-iron foot. No Jerome this morning. Ran-dull instead . . . will have to settle for second best . . . not the best start, but J will make do!! Fugaz. What is the game for today? Tony."

The bus slithers along its usual path, people board, Jaime looks up periodically to see if any of them catch his eye: a few girls who were once classmates of Teresita's or Tony's and who are now cradling babies in their arms or in strollers; a few teenagers his age, none at his middle school, boisterous, listening to hip-hop or dance-hall blaring from headset speakers, their backpacks rattling with drug paraphernalia, perhaps, or forties; an old woman, dressed in a filthy white blouse and yellow shorts, a pink hairnet framing a face drooping like melting brown wax; another older woman, white and in an appliquéd blue frock, yammering excitedly to herself; an older man, maybe forty-five, somewhere Uncle Narciso's age, in a red and white striped polo shirt, brown polyester beltless pants, and matching brown buckled loafers. He slides into the row of seats across from Jaime and smiles. Jaime acknowledges him, almost absently.

Light is now flooding the bus. May sun. The fragrances of sandalwood, a cologne that must be Brut and newsprint commingle in Jaime's consciousness: he turns slowly towards the man who has a full head of graying wavy hair and an almost lacquered black mustache. The man pulls out the sports section of his newspaper and starts reading the back-page write-up of last night's big boxing match, which Teresita and Eric and his mother had been watching on pay-per-view. *My hurt.* Jaime had instead been printing out his index cards, and had telephoned Vinh with a question about one of the languages in Senegal, which Vinh of course knew about. They had spoken for about twenty minutes. *My love.* Vinh was in the midst of doing what he spends all of his free time doing, like Jaime: reading or drawing.

Jaime examines the man more carefully. He must be still in his forties, because although gray salts his hair, his face does not look *that* old. Skinny almost, he has a complexion not unlike Jaime's own, the color of an unshelled almond; and thick lips, like Jaime's father, like Corey, like Jaime. Through the small triangle created by the placket of his shirt, Jaime can almost see the hairless chest. It looks like it may be toned; the man cranes slightly forward, obscuring Jaime's view. Jaime watches him study the scores, and draws a picture of him. What does he do all day, who is he, where is he going? Jaime writes these questions down, in order. *If I were myself, but like Tony: What would I do? What would he do?* As Jaime scribbles, the bus stops, people board, de-board.

When Jaime looks out of the bus window for a change, he sees a fourteen-year-old girl he knows, named Mercedes, whom they call Dita, in front of the liquor store, stepping out of a fire-engine-red Samurai with two boys, from a gang that hangs out at Four Corners. He bows his head so that he can watch her unobserved, though it is unlikely she even notices the bus's presence. She had wanted to have Tony's baby so badly, just a year ago, but since Tony's death, Jaime has rarely seen her. One of the men wraps his arm around Dita's waist, eases his hand down the side of her leg, slides it over onto her behind . . .

Jaime turns back to the man, who has been staring at him.

The man gets up and slides in next to Jaime, who pushes his knapsack against the window. *What does he do all day, who is he, where is he going?*

—Hhhiiih . . . , Jaime says, his voice breathy and tremulous, like a vibrating reed.

—Hey, the man replies. How you doing this morning? His voice is pure ice.

—Fine.

—Tha's good, the man says, baring his straight, yellowing smile. Jaime spots the wedding band on his left ring finger, which, like all the others, is long, unwrinkled, and spoonlike. Maybe he is younger than Uncle Narciso. Setting the paper in his lap, the man slowly examines the riders on the bus, his head angling and turning as if it were a movie camera. Jaime searches the bus for anyone who might call him out. Corey is still up front, but he is now conversing intensely with one of the young mothers. The man appears to mime placing his hand on Jaime's knee, but does not. He simply looks down at Jaime and smiles. The teeth gleam like butter-covered knives. Jaime can feel his underarms beginning to moisten. *My son.*

—Where you headed? the man asks.

—Wha's your name? Jaime answers.

—I like that, 'What's your name?'... My name is Vernon, what's yours? He lays a hand on the seatback next to Jaime's shoulders. Jaime licks his palms and sweeps back his curls; this man's name cannot *really* be Vernon, Jaime tells himself; he must be playing a game as well. He looks out into the traffic alongside the bus: cars snake past on their way to wherever.

—Tony.

—Tony... Where you headed, Tony?

—Cuffe School... Where you headed?

—Nowhere, I got the day off...

Vernon purses his lips, then asks, —Tony, why don't we get off at the next stop? I'll walk you partway there. We can talk. He smiles again, as the fingers, like the petals of some exquisite brown flower, flutter out upon the seatback. Jaime inhales deeply, his mind swirling with questions: What *is* happening? Who is this man? Where are they going? Is he going to miss *algebra*? Because Mr. Morris will surely telephone his mother and admonish him in front of the class. The bus halts at the stop, and they both slip out through the back door. As the bus pulls away, Jaime reminds himself that although he has never taken a game *this far,* Vernon seems decent enough, and Jaime decides that, no matter what, he will *not* act as he normally would.

The sidewalk flares with the morning heat. Sun glints off every

metal surface in dazzling spars, forcing Jaime to put on the pair of
sunglasses he keeps in the front pocket of his backpack. Vernon
dons a pair, too; where had he stored them? At the green light,
they cross the street together, walking quickly, almost in tandem,
then walk several blocks up before turning into a side street,
where they pause. Jaime's hands, like Vernon's, are pocketed. He
scans the main street to see if anyone he knows is passing by. Not
a soul.

Pointing in the direction of the projects, to their left, Vernon
tells Jaime, —Now, if I'm correct, Cuffe is about six blocks that
way. Jaime wrinkles his lips several times, then nods in agreement.

Running his hand over the lip of his pants, Vernon continues,
—Cuffe School, Cuffe School...I remember when the Cuffe
School first became the Cuffe School. Used to be Wendell Phillips
School when my kids went there, then they decided to change the
name. Always do. Can't leave well enough alone. Can't say I actually know who Cuffe is, you know...or Wendell Phillips for that
matter. I guess you kids don't care who it's named after, though,
hunh?

All this talk annoys Jaime, who says nervously, —No, no,
nobody cares. He brushes the hair back from his forehead: Vernon is plumper than Jaime thought, or perhaps it is just that he
has a gut like Uncle Narciso; he begins to wonder if he should not
just run off, end this game right now, wait till after school, another day...What time is it anyway? he wonders.

—Turn around so I can see how *handsome* you are. You are so
handsome, you know? Jaime follows the instructions, revolving in
a gradual circle. Vernon now looks older than he did at first, on
the bus; the sunlight colors in the slight sagging of his chin, the
almost slack quality of the skin on his arms, like a sheet of crumpled brown plastic. He is definitely older than *Tío*.

—How old are you, Tony?

—How old are *you*, Vernon?

—There you go again, answering my question with another
question. My age doesn't matter, Tony, but I'm forty-nine. Now,
how old are you?

Jaime throws his head back, closes his eyes, says casually, —I'm sixteen and a half. I got kept back a few times and I look young for my age.

Beginning to laugh, Vernon inspects Jaime up and down. —Now, Tony, I ain't no *fool*. I think you're about thirteen, maybe fourteen. Either way, this could turn into a crime in the state of Massachusetts, you know that? Jaime remains silent, fiddling anxiously with his Day-Glo wristband, which is now primed with sweat. *My heart.*

—Look, if you're gonna call me a liar, I can just leave.

Vernon flashes those teeth again in a furious grin. —Who said anything like that, about you being a liar? We cool, ain't we, Tony?

—Anyways, if I did leave, where would that leave *you*? Jaime bats his eyes, turning his back to Vernon. This, he thinks, is not going where he thought it would, though he is unsure where that was.

Vernon moves closer to Jaime and rests his hand on the boy's shoulder. —Why don't we take a walk behind that old filling station there? I knew the man who owned it, you know, Vernon whispers, his voice trailing off. Jaime reminds himself just because they go back there, nothing really *has to* occur. It's a game; he's *Tony,* this man is playing along, nothing will happen. He also thinks if Tony were alive and he knew about this, he would put his gun to this man's temple right now and pull the trigger until the clip was completely emptied so that the eyes and snot mixed into the ground like spilled soup and then stomp on the head until the face was unrecognizable. So unrecognizable *that no one could figure out who he was but Jaime had known instantly, just by that scent;* instead that very thing happened to Tony and now he is lying six feet under a headstone in a cemetery in Jamaica Plain, his face shattered into a hundred pieces like a porcelain doll, his body so twisted that they could barely fit the suit on him, and no one is here to stop this game, stop it at all, save Jaime from anything, from *himself,* no one cares, not his mother not his father not his aunts or uncles or sisters not Teresita not Tita not even his *abuela,* no one, the only one who ever cared and showed it is silent and silenced for posterity so why not see what is going to happen this morning—

They head down an oil-slicked gravel driveway toward the rear of the abandoned gas station, which abuts a narrow alley, bordered on three sides by a brick wall, covered by ivy and other climbing vines. Jaime has passed by this site before, though he has never actually ventured back in here.

Vernon leans against the back wall of the station. He unbuckles his pants. Jaime faces him, his eyes now falling everywhere but on Vernon, who has begun to expose himself, urging the boy to approach him. Is this part of the game? Jaime asks without rendering the words audible, fixed to his spot. What would *Tony* do? His eyes still wandering, his mind leaping alternately from Vernon's extended fingers to Tony's veined brown hands gripping that 9mm—that's what it was, wasn't it, a 9mm, a Tech-Nine pulling the trigger again again again, him finding the body back behind the Dumpster behind the store like garbage dumped in the middle of the night, his mother not able to say anything at all for days, her lying on the floor beneath the pew convulsing in tears at the funeral, him under his comforter shivering in the overheated room, working himself into a frenzy at the sight of that body, that horrible corpse, that face mangled beyond recognition, beyond even hideousness, as the bed across from him lies empty empty empty—

—Com'ere, Tony, Vernon clucks, his eyes closed and his body arched back against the wall. Jaime approaches until he is standing in front of him, stone-still. That's *good*. Jaime just stands there, his eyes now fixed on Vernon's hairless and pocked torso, paler than his face or arms, like the flesh of a plucked chicken, which he has revealed by raising his polo shirt. Jaime tenses as the hand clamps onto his shoulder. Tony! Vernon is hunching over, breathing heavily. Turn around for me again, Tony! Tony?

Jaime, who feels himself slowly losing his sense of balance-distance-time letting everything go why can't he concentrate why can't he be a man like Tony would why can't he end this game end it now get closer to Vernon run why why why is this happening like this why is this happening he begins to turn look down find the head crumpled like a toy doll fall shoot convulsed in tears my god why my *son* on the floor of the pew why my God *por qué* when he hears, —Oh, Tony...Tony, *ooooh*...

He opens his eyes suddenly. What time *is* it? Vernon's left hand is massaging Jaime's shoulder, his right hand...he feels his chest collapsing. He glimpses Vernon's watch on his right hand...he's late for his algebra class! He is going to *miss* it! Jaime leaps up, stumbles backwards, knocking over his knapsack, spilling the contents upon the stones.

—Wha? Hunh? Vernon murmurs, writhing against the wall like a felled bird struggling to alight, riven with bliss, unaware of the boy's actions. Panicking, Jaime snatches up his knapsack, stuffs everything back in it, hoists it onto his left shoulder, hesitates. *My life*, he feels rising on the tip of his tongue: No one is going to save him from anything, ever, *not a soul*.

—Wha's the matter, Tony? *Tony?* Jaime, refusing to look in Vernon's direction, runs off down the driveway, his backpack now half-open and dangling from his back. In about five seconds he is onto the street that leads through the projects and into the front door of the Cuffe Middle School, pass the hall monitor who is yelling out his name—*Jaime Barrett, Jaime Barrett, Jaime?*—up onto the third floor, into a seat in the back of the class as Mr. Morris is chalking a series of dizzyingly elaborate equations upon the black slate that appears now as depthless as the voice that is explaining the actions of the hand and chalk, and Jaime, in the back row, is fumbling around madly in his bag, his hands searching furiously for that algebra notebook—where *is* it? He *knows* he packed it, he remembers having placed it in there this morning—which is *nowhere* to be found.

Then he sees it, he sees it as keenly as if it all were unreeling right before him, *here:* As Vernon gets ready to depart, he spots a notebook, lying several inches in front of him. A black and white wirebound gridded notebook, which has ALGEBRA I—MR. MORRIS, FIRST PERIOD etched across its front. Picking up the notebook, he flips through it, seeing all the red marks and the heavily annotated margins of the pages, which, like a used scratch-and-sniff sample held close to the nose, emit a faint but perceptible scent: sandalwood. He casts the notebook to the ground, beside the discarded newspaper, laughs at the folly of it all, at this boy who cannot even keep up his role in their game, walks off down the driveway towards Dudley and the rest of his life—

His bangs now plastered like a veil to his forehead, his breathing so labored as to drown out even his own thoughts, Jaime looks up, to the puzzled expressions of Mr. Morris, of Vinh, of every student in his algebra class. Their faces are screens of bemusement, showing only the recognition of his strange and novel presence before them. Their eyes have fixed upon him as if he were the last boy on earth, their stares as blank and unrelenting as if they had never seen such a pitiful and enigmatic creature in their entire lives.

Ogoni

Neighbors, please don't
  mind me this morning
    at windows balling my fists

at the sun. Lowdown
  bastards, imbeciles
    & infidels, a tribunal

of jackasses behind
  mirrored sunglasses
    with satchels of loot—wait,

calm down, count to twenty
  & take a few deep breaths.
    You don't want to disgrace

his heroic tongue. Go
  to the kitchen window
    & sit in that chair

striped like a zebra,
  & imagine how a herd runs
    with an oscillating rhythm,

like a string bass & drums
  trading riffs. The big cats
    can only see a striped hill

moving beneath a sunset,
  a grid of grass & trees
    in motion, a pattern to fear

& instinct, because they run
    as one, as sky & earth. Look
        at the scrappy robin & blue jay

squabble over earthworms
    underneath the ginkgo,
        as a boy on the edge

of memory raises a Daisy
    air rifle. Look at the robin
        puff out its bright chest

like a bull's-eye. Only
    a cocky boy could conjure
        a ricochet in his head

that hits a horseshoe
    looped around an iron peg,
        a little of God's geometry

to get things perfect.
    A single red leaf
        spirals to the ground.

Where did the birds
    go, now why am I
        weeping at this window?

That's not my face
    strung to the hands
        holding the gun, unmasked

by the Shell trademark
    on his gold money clip,
        worms throbbing behind

the scab grown over
his eyes. Those damn
bastards murdered a good man

when they killed Ken
Saro-Wiwa. Why was he so
cool, did the faces of his

wife & children steady
his voice? "I predict
the denouncement of the riddle

of the Niger delta
will soon come." Did
you feel dead grass quiver

& birds stop singing?
To cut the acid rage
& put some sugar

back on the tongue,
I'll say my wife's name
forever—the only song

I'm willing to beat
myself up a hill for,
to die with in my mouth.

Letters

"Dear Muzz," I wrote, the summer I was ten
from a seedy nature camp in the Poconos
with cows and calves, huge geese, some half-wild ponies
—heaven for the urban savage I was then—
"I have to do this letter to get breakfast.
Kiss Kerry for me. I milked a cow named Clover."
(Kerry, my dog, already dead, run over
the week I left.) Muzz from the bosomy British
matron in charge of spunky orphans who reclaim
the family's fortunes in a book I adored.
My older brothers called you Dolly, cleared
as almost-adults to use your cute nickname.
"Dear Muzz, with love" however smudged and brief
from your animal, sole daughter in your life.

Your animal, sole daughter in your life,
I mourned my dog, the slaughter of Clover's calf.
You were born Bella, number six of twelve.
The butter was spread too thin, childhood too brief
shared with Eva, Sara, Lena, Esther, Saul,
Meyer, Nathan, Oscar, Dan, Jay, Joe.
The younger ones mewed to be held by you.
The older ones, above your crib, said "doll."
You made me your confessor. At eighteen
you eloped, two virgins fleeing Baltimore,
buttoned in one berth by a Pullman porter
who jollied your tears at breakfast next morning
before the train pulled into Buffalo.
Your face announced Just Married, you blushed so.

Just married, one day pregnant, you blushed so
pink Niagara's fabled sunset paled.

"Papa will kill me when he hears," you quailed
but the first grandchild, a boy, softened the blow.
You told me how your mother had slapped your face
the day your first blood caked along your thighs,
then sent you to your sister for advice.
Luckier, I was given *Marjorie May's*
Twelfth Birthday, a vague tract printed by Kotex,
so vague it led me to believe you bled
that one year only, and chastely left unsaid
the simple diagrammatics about sex.
When was it that I buried Muzz, began
to call you by the name that blazoned Woman?

I came to call you Dolly, The Other Woman,
the one I couldn't be. I was cross-eyed,
clumsy, solitary, breasts undersized.
Made wrong. An orthodontist's dream. A bookworm.
That winter, a house guest, his wife gone shopping,
pinned me in my bedroom by the mirror
and as we both watched, took out to my horror
a great stiff turkey neck, a hairless thing
he wanted to give me. How could I tell you this,
how he pressed against me, put it in my hand,
groped my nipples, said, "Someday you'll understand"?
How tell you, who couldn't say vagina, penis?
This isn't recovered memory. I never forgot it.
I came to call you Dolly. That's when it started.

At fourteen, I called you Dolly. The war had started,
absorbing my brothers one by one. The first-
born fought in Rommel's Africa, then crossed
to the Italian boot. Your cocktail parties
grew shriller that year, the air more fiercely mortal
as the second son went off to ferry bombers
over the Burma hump. Your hair, by summer,
began to thin, then fell out, purgatorial.
The youngest, apple of your eye, was shot
down in the Pacific, plucked from his atoll

and survived with a pair of shattered ankles.
You had to wear a wig. I dared to gloat.
The rage of adolescence bit me deep.
I loathed your laugh, your scarves, your costly makeup.

Your laugh, your scarves, the gloss of your makeup,
shallow and vain. I wore your lips, your hair,
even the lift of my eyebrows was yours
but nothing of you could please me, bitten so deep
by the fox of scorn. Like you, I married young
but chose animals, wood heat, hard hours
instead of Sheffield silver, fresh-cut flowers,
your life of privilege and porcelain.
Then children came, the rigorous bond of blood.
Little by little our lives pulled up, pulled even.
A sprinkle here and there of approbation:
we both agreed that what I'd birthed was good.
How did I come to soften? How did you?
Goggy is what my little ones called you.

Goggy, they called you, basking in the sun
of your attention. You admired their ballet;
their French; their algebra; their Bach and Debussy.
The day the White House rang you answered, stunned
your poet-daughter was wanted on the phone
—the Carters' party for a hundred bards.
We shopped together for the dress I'd wear.
Our rancors melted as ocean eases stone.
That last year of your life, the names you thought of:
Rogue, Doc, Tudor, Daisy, Garth,
the horses of your lost Virginia youth.
You said them, standing in my barn, for love.
Dying, you scratched this fragment for me, a prize;
"Darling...your visit...even...so brief...Muzz."

ADRIAN C. LOUIS

Earth Bone Connected to the Spirit Bone

Where is the Life we lost in living?
—T. S. Eliot

When America died, I was passed out and I never noticed. Was it a meteor or an invisible wand that waved past our eyes and blinded everyone? I awoke one morning and electrical maggots were spurting from the mind-control machine in our disheveled living room. We are off the Rez in Rushville, Nebraska, eighteen miles from Pine Ridge. Under the carcinogenic mist of the cropdusters, this lame-brained bordertown staggers and smiles. There is only one restaurant—at the bowling alley—and it has skanky, subhuman food. The high school team is nicknamed "The Longhorns." The steaks and hamburger in the largest grocery store in town are Third World. This is the heart of cattle country. A ripened, diseased American heart.

From eighteen miles south, I watch the Rez gangbangers come to town—pallid, goofy reflections of the gang scum they've seen on TV. Sedated by sweating daylight, they rise to moonlight's murderous soul. Broken, the sacred circle is. Broken, the sacred circle is light years from mending. We all play Indian roulette. Red fluid of life. Black fluid of death. My wheel spins into middle-aged sameness. Still, there is something I want to say about love. It is the cruelest drug and I have used and abused it. And now I am spinning, afraid to die alone or together. And we are all the same, even our leaders, the tribal politicians. Our chiefs are big, brown ants in panties. Flint-skinned mutants of the sacred song. Insects. Hear me. Where is my HUD house? Where are our warriors? Where are the ancestor spirits who should be guiding us? Where is the love?

O Reservation. Home, home, hell. Eighteen miles north resides our howl and hovel where everything changes except the rusty bars across the moon. Listen, listen to the rabid coyote in the frozen Badlands. It is singing a love song to us. A wild-ass cowboy and Indian tune. We can still hear it at this Nebraska Street

Dance. Yeeeeeee-hawwwww! Cowpokes all over the butt-fucking place. Huge, hairy galoots, veritable Blutos under straw Stetsons. On horses by day, on heifers tonight.

· · ·

And glimmering in the eastern mist is Oz—no, I mean Lincoln, Nebraska. Beyond green cornfields that white city gleams. Midwestern Cambridge. Home of *Cliffs Notes*. City of lame, homespun poets and other plains jokers. The catapult where state income taxes launch Huskers to Orange Bowls. Great American city with a parched cornfield soul: O rasping, generic America. Home of the hospital we visit and leave with pills to flower false hope.

· · ·

You are upstairs on your Prozac and Haldol. I'm forty-eight years old and groggy from napping after self-flagellation. The two Bible thumpers at the front door graze on my nakedness. God help me if you can, I mumble at them. I am scaling the black glass canyons of hell and doing tolerably well, almost enjoying myself as they titter and quickly turn whiter than white.

· · ·

God bless our Indian democracy. The red sun rises. Since the diagnosis, neither of us work. The bathtub is yellow. The bills are white. They mount and mount as do my collection of books. Writers I don't know send me their books from every corner of this mad nation. I am too busy caring for you to read. Our fieldstone basement is crumbling under the weight of their books. I wish they would send money, not books.

· · ·

You have taken to wandering. Vanished for the third time this month. You are out there someplace shimmering in your own haze of dead memory. It does no good to call the cops. I've learned my lesson. Twice they've brought you back from the video store. I sit and wait for your return, trying the mindless anesthetic of MTV. I watch the music in black and white. In Seattle, young grunge nihilists are experiencing impotence before their time. In L.A., young black rappers sing grunts of the vengeful cock—a self-demonizing sort of urban Mandingo lingo that reservation kids are now mouthing, too. Rap scares me. How is it possible to age with grace? Where is the desperado I was? Where are you now, my love? And how is it still possible for me to hate? Worn by the daily agitation of your slow-motion, terminal disease, I retain my anger. I turn off the tube and I think of one enemy in particular. The bastard is thirteen years older than me and I will not be speaking ill of the dead when I piss on his grave. I will be merely dousing the white devils which possessed him. Their names were greed, success, material goods, and Jesus H. Christ.

. . .

Still waiting, I call my friend Simon to see if he's seen her. He asks to borrow money. He needs medicine to get well, but no, no money, Cousin. You already owe me. No, I ain't giving you no twelve-step quick-step. Only the bottom, hard, harsh, and swift. Then you get up or don't, either one better than now. Oh, how you love living death. Oh, how you live loving death. Simon said he fell down and broke his crown and awoke at the VA hospital in a room filled with decrepit old men in wheelchairs. "I was one of them," he said and chuckled.

So I then said to Simon: "The information superhighway leads to consciousness overflowing the toilet *or* true denial. The murderous nature of man craves Nature's death. I know where you're coming from. Every day I also fight the urge to drink. Every minute of every day. Sometimes I think: What if I got cancer? If I did, the first one to know would be a bartender. I'd be just like you." And after an insufferable silence, Simon said at least he wasn't coughing up blood, but he did go into seizures: "The earth was dying—and its children, too. The earth was dying—and its children, too."

. . .

I'm sweating bullets at the Social Security office in the nearest large city. This homely white woman's got me bent over her desk and is banging me good. No, we're not legally married, I tell her. No, I'm not her legal guardian. Just approve the damn papers, please. Christ!—I just wish someone would have asked this bureaucrat to her high school prom. These gray-faced government mutants are all the slime-fucking-same. Hey, their souls are powdered milk and we are the water they crave. In this hallucination of midlife, I whitewash all fatalistic interrogatives. There is no primeval carnage of carcasses in caves. The black crust entombing blood lies upon a sesame seed bun. I am plastic America. I am the holy man among the hollow men who worship at the altar of greed. For many years I possessed the true Holy Grail and drank beer from it. Now I am the toad Prince. Kiss me and fuck me till I'm raw, darling dearest fed employee, but God please approve the paperwork.

· · ·

I come and go like the pavement in winter. No longer grease-black at the intersection of blood leaves and salt-peppered snow, I sometimes dye my sideburns, my soul. Smirking ancestors appear and disappear. My dogs are turning gray and swimming slowly throughout the house. There were many women I loved, but I think they all had the same name. I love you. I love you. They were all you and now you are slowly vanishing. Vanishing.

From a bleached fence post aimed at the gunpowder sky, an eagle explodes upward. Our car is speeding down the ice road when we see a small plume dancing earthward. Your circle is almost full. That is the message of the feather, yet I continue to pretend that I don't understand it. This dreadful curse of middle age is no joking matter. I'm no longer young and my mind can't grasp that fact. There is not one truth, but many truths. There are no lies—just fearful shadings of the truth. I learned all my banks. I learned all the English I needed in eight ball and snooker.

This, thus, is what I learned. You are dying and you are not dying. I wish I could have you do the rest. This is your poem. Here are the words, this is the vision. Hey, this *is* the poem. Ride it if you can. All your worlds are vanishing. I am not sad, but it is getting hard to love you. Do you understand? Do you? I remember your father said, "Long as I can remember, us Indians leased our land to the white man." He said, "The *wasicu* grows hay and gets rich." He used to run circles around these round bales when he was a kid getting in shape for high school basketball—the famed 1936 State Champs. He said, "Sometimes, just at dusk, these bales look like ghosts of the buffalos or . . . something, you know?" Now he is dead.

· · ·

Darling, it seems my only reason for living is to help you remember. Do you recall that white man who said how come at every powwow you honor the American flag? This has always been a puzzle to me, he said. You are the people who fell through the crack in the Liberty Bell. You are always the first to invoke the Washita River or Bosque Redondo or Wounded Knee when you perceive injustice against your people. God, despite the centuries of atrocities this country committed against you Indian people, you still love to honor that flag. I just don't get it, the white man said to us.

There was no way to answer him. What could we say? Someone said Sitting Bull said:

If the Great Spirit had desired me to be a white man, he would have made me so in the first place.

It is not necessary for eagles to be crows.

Most of us know Sitting Bull wasn't bullshitting, but we still don't know which way to go. We are torn between two different worlds and between the past and the future. At least that's what we tell ourselves when we fail. We never mention the fact that it was Indians who killed Mr. Bull.

. . .

On Sundays the caterwauling from this bordertown church down the street is fearless, fearful, fearsome. In that eternal fear they call Christian love, they yodel to forget who they are and screech the wondrous lie that all of us are their God's children. If their God is real, why doesn't he help us? We are paying taxes here, too. It is all a bland joke. I have heard these same poor whites say Skins don't want to work and curse us, sputtering that if it weren't for the government handouts, we'd starve to death. And on Friday nights I've seen flocks of these same angel-addled sodbusters drunk and desperate for Indian pussy and worse. Last winter a mid-February thaw startled cows into dropping early calves onto the muddy plains. Even trees were tricked into budding. That week a cop in Gordon, Nebraska, murdered an Indian guy. Shot him square in the back and got away with it.

When I was young I could always tell who the real cowboys were. They always smelled like cowshit. These days they wear nylon panties under their jeans and draw their guns as if their redneck lives had meaning. Damn this chapped-ass cowboy hell. Damn this cowturd state of mind, this verbal puke, this pain.

      . . .

Once the Rez sun rose bloated and angered. Like a neglected child, it pouted over the purple hills surrounding Pine Ridge Village. Dogs ran looking for cars to crush them. Soon it would be too hot to do anything but find shade and suffer, yet Adrian would survive. He had enough beer stocked up to get drunk and sleep through the heat of the day and get drunk again at night. Adrian was one smart Indian alkie. A flesh and blood oxymoron. O sweetheart, remember?

      . . .

Note to a young Rez writer:

    Hey, Cuz, I thought they were eagles circling above, a sign of good luck for Skins, but closer inspection revealed them to be the turkey vultures of broken English. Hey, Cuz, I remember once you sent me a hand-scrawled note saying you were out of typewriter ribbons and I sent you off fifty bucks that same day and you wrote back saying you got the ribbons and some Big Macs to boot. Young brother, now I am saddened down to the core of my sour-wine soul. Young brother. Young brother. You've become famous before your time.

      . . .

My ancient mower refuses to eat any more lawn. It belches and farts and quits. The rusty steel teeth have had their fill. Sweating dusk sedates me so I nap on the couch and wake to the pine-goosed moon. With aching old muscles and a young heart slightly crazed by my own funk and thirst, I head out for the Stockman's Saloon in Rushville, Nebraska. It is quiet there when I walk in and order a nonalcohol beer and an *Omaha World-Herald*. In this newspaper made from blood of trees, I read about Johnnie Cochran and Marcia Clark in Los Angeles. I have lived in that mutant world of concrete canyons. The bartender says L.A. deserves a thermonuclear enema. He is white and has green teeth. Me, I'd vote for Las Vegas or Nazi Serbia.

      . . .

The pale professor who claimed to be Cherokee was spelunking in baleen. When she decried the whiteness of the whale and scrimshawed the blackboard, my sad soul tittered at her blubber butt jiggling. The poor woman would never see that Melville's big fish was an Indian whale. I should've let her taste the ripe redness of my hapless harpoon. Yippie-ki-yi-yo. I should've bowed, kissed her hand, and whispered that before he shipped out with Ahab, Queequeg had his lonely sperm frozen. And that I am one of his clones. Screw it all. I have written this several times before, but again I say that downtown, inside the Rez post office, a poster displays new stamps: romantic Indian war bonnets in hues never seen by our ancestors. Outside, bruised and bumbling winos trod by with Hefty bags full of flattened cans. Again I say that when Crazy Horse was murdered at Fort Robinson, the last living free Indian died. Except for me, darling. Except for me, sweetheart. All my life I have been young and this year I no longer am. The summer is putrid and I'm toying with six years of good behavior. Sweating and drinking near beer, I'm in the oven of a bordertown bar and I don't know why I crawled in. Maybe it has something to do with courage but the air is harsh and purple. I'm wedged in a narrow passage and it's purple-black and scurrying sounds are dancing in the darkness. I know Jehovah is dead so I'm praying to the television, yes, goddamn it, I'm praying to Phil Donahue that I won't start drinking:

Help me, Phil. Let me free to be me! I'm an Indian morsel trapped in the guts of a cannibal called America who, for rabid religious reasons and a touch of trickle-down economics, has shoved a pickle past its tight sphincters. I don't want to drink. No I don't, so help me, Phil. Clinch your lust-mongering, liberal fangs upon that dill, Phil, and yank the mother out.

. . .

Earth bone connected to the spirit bone. That's what I say in the chest-pain night. Heart bone connected to the ghost bone! And I pray that I could take all the imposed infirmities of flesh, all the little cancers, the tooth cavities, the blackheads, the failing kidneys, the wrinkling skin, the allergies, the aphasia, take all those bad things from one's body, suck them out by cosmic means, compress all those negatives into a compact ball of black star mass and hurl it into the sun. Then they would all pay...I mean pray. And the molten-golden dew of love would cover this land. But life is not so TV-easy. We cannot remove decay. Still, it is the wish of newness we desire. Like, if everything in our worn house could automatically become new: the sunken couch arises, the flickering TV becomes clear, the dog-stained rug becomes immaculate, and the walls are freshly painted...but life is not so TV-easy. And no. No molten-golden dew of love will ever cover this land.

Ponce de Leon was not searching for gold when he came trudging up the Everglades humming papal torture songs. We know that he was searching for the "fountain of youth." And so what (in my hours of darkness, when the computer of memory scrolls your ancient flashbacks) do I focus on, wish a return to? A moment of stolen sex, or an accidental hand-touching, or a wistful glance of some unrequited love? Maybe a touchdown pass in a high school football game? No! For the most part, I seem to want to return to pained points of failure. Earth bone connected to the spirit bone, indeed...and often the doors of memory are of no consequence.

I, Adrian, live in the land of the common doorbell. Every time the doorbell rings on a TV commercial, my dogs go wild and I jump up off the couch looking for a place to hide. Me, a middle-aged man acting like it's 1962: I'm a sophomore in high school, it's Saturday, and I'm in my cubbyhole of a room off the enclosed porch of the old railroad shack whacking off and the dogs start barking and I see a pickup churning up our dirt road. I am in my sanctuary, connecting my groin bone to the heaven bone. I do not worry until there is a pounding on the small pine door to my room. My Nutty-Putty heart ricochets around my half-breed rib cage. I pull up my pegged Levi's and peek out the door. There is Chris Brandon, fellow soph but a white boy, dressed in his usual, starched, button-down clothes. I smell the Vitalis on his flat-top with wings. He is no friend, only someone I pass in the halls, but what the hell is he doing here? On the porch outside my room is a bucket of soiled diapers from one of my little sisters. The entire corridor is swamped with shit-smell. The whole house is in dirty disarray. Burning shame makes my eyeballs flutter. In the living room I can see my illiterate, drunken white stepfather making small talk with Brandon's father. My brown mother is scurrying after the smaller kids and she's wearing a tattered gingham dress.

Her black hair is electric and she's pregnant although the baby she's holding is less than a year old and the flypaper above my head is so covered with flies that it couldn't hold another, and worst of all, I've still got a boner, and Brandon looks down and spots it. At that instant I pray for nuclear attack. A complete devastation of mankind, of Adrian, of Brandon, of my entire known world existing in the midst of that Nevada Indian poverty thirty-three years ago. So, now I live in the land of the common doorbell. I live in the land of the common death. This is still Indian country and it is to the Indian spirits that I must pray. I must fill our home with prayer. Death and madness are hovering above our house. And I have the need of prayer. Earth bone connected to the spirit bone. I must pray for the woman I love. Her very mind is vanishing. I must burn sweet grass, sage, and pray with the pipe. And so I pray:

Grandfather of the West—
In the setting sun of my birth, in the red blood air of my birth, I am praying to you. Pity me. Help me, please. Help me to help another whose mind is evaporating like rain on these July plains. Help me to help another who truly needs my help. With this first clump of tobacco into the pipe I pray for her.

Grandfather of the North—
Grandfather of this land of the pines and cold winds. Take pity on me. I do not pray for myself. I am praying for wholeness for all of us thus fractured. We are many, Grandfather. We are ghost warriors in the setting sun, an endless army of broken Skins. This second clump of tobacco goes in the pipe.

Grandfather of the East—
Who lives where the sun rises and darkness is eased. This third clump is for you. Again, I pray for wholeness and for sanity. I pray for another who needs your help. I pray for a woman who needs your healing. She is a good woman, your Indian daughter. She has made her mistakes, but her heart is good. Upon all that is holy, I say she is kind. Upon all that is holy, she deserves to be whole.

Grandfather of the South—
One toward whom we all face. I pray for wholeness and good health for someone I love dearly. This is not a prayer for myself. Please listen, Grandfather. This fourth clump of tobacco for you. Help her, please.

Grandfather, who is the Great Spirit—
One who I call *Numanah,* and my woman calls *Tunkasila,* I pray to you. You are the Creator, you are the Great Spirit. You are our God. Pity me. Help me. Help me to be a good, strong man to an ailing woman. This fifth clump is to open your ears.

Grandmother Earth—
Mother of us all. I pray to you, I pray for your feminine assistance. Pity me. Help me. Help me to help one of your daughter-sisters. And now the pipe is loaded. Now it is ready to be smoked. And now a second round of prayers. It is needed. Dear spirits, it is needed.

O Spirits of the West Wind—
Receive this pipe and have pity on your people. From you comes the Thunderbird who purifies the *inipi* and the earth. You correct our mistakes. We are frail and weak humans and we sometimes do not do things right. You keep us from doing wrong. You are the giver of rain and the beginning of life. The thunder of your Horse People from the Black Mountains fills us with awe. You are mighty. Send the Black Eagle to help us. We await your arrival.

Spirits of the North—
You live in the sacred Red Mountains. From you comes the good, red road—the holy road of our people. It is with you the Sacred Buffalo Calf Woman stands. It is you who lead the Buffalo People out of lost darkness. Help me be strong and steady under this adversity. Enable me to walk the good, red road with a straight face. Let me not talk out of both sides of my mouth. Let me truly be humble and honest. Show me the starlight path that leads to the good land. Send your messenger, the Golden Eagle, to guide

us. Help me as I pray to you with your sacred pipe. I am praying for one I love who, in her frailty, needs my love and strength.

Spirits of the East—
From you comes the Morning Star which radiates wisdom. From you comes the sun filling our dark world with light. From you comes the moon that gives us help and protection at night. In your Yellow Mountains the powerful Elk People shake their great horns. Send the Bald Eagle and help me gain wisdom that I may find the things to do and say to help the one I love. This is my need. This is what I pray for.

Spirits of the South—
Land where all living things face, where all the animal spirits live, have pity on me, and turn your face toward me. Send your messenger, the White Crane. Help me, in my need, help me to help the one I love. Help me to be strong for her and not against her. Let not my fear turn into anger. Let my love fly into her heart. Hear me, O Spirits of the South.

Grandfather, Great Spirit—
Have pity on the lowly piece of crap that I am. Accept this humility as my true state and not some conjured prayer stick. You are powerful and above all things. All things come from you. You are the most holy. You are the most holy. Let your Spotted Eagle look down upon me and hear my prayer. You can do all things. Help me in my need to help the one I love.

Grandmother Earth—
It is from you that we come, and it is to your arms that one day we shall return. From you comes all our food and all that grows. From you comes the medicine plants, the winged creatures, the four-legged, the things that swim and crawl. Grandmother, help me for I am pitiful. It is to your arms that one day we shall return, Grandmother, but for the one I love this is not the time. Spirits, I smoke this pipe and pray to you. My earth bone is connected to your spirit bone. *Mitakuye oyas'in.* For all my relations, but for one in particular.

And so it begins or ends...If I am not prayer, at least the prayer has been launched. Earth bone connected to the spirit bone. The rest is up to the spirits. I listen to the ghost talk of tumbleweeds, nightcrawling, rasping across the dry desert heart of my distant homelands. I listen and listen, but there is no real amen. A word comes, an English word with harsh Germanic overtones. A solitary word comes and erases the connection between earth bone and spirit bone. That word is Teutonic and Nazi-sounding. That word is Alzheimer's.

And now, fuck all the words I've ever uttered, it becomes the only word in our world.

Heartsong

A bird sings from the tree. The birds sing
sending waves of desire—and I stand on my roof
waiting for a randomness to storm my days. I stand on my roof
filled with the longing that sings its way out of the bird.
And I am afraid that my call will break me,
that the cry blocked by my tongue will pronounce me mad.
O bird mad with longing, O balancing bar,
tightrope, monkey grunting from a roof. Fortunate bird.
I stand on my roof and wave centuries of desire.
I am the Bedouin pondering the abandoned campsite
licking the ashes of the night fire; the American walking
walking miles of dresses, blouses, and skirts
filling them with infinite lovers;
the mystic feeling the pull swirling in his chest,
a desert of purpose expanding and burning and yellowing
every shade of green. And I stand on my roof.
And I say come like a stranger, like a feather
falling on an old woman's shoulder, like a hawk
that comes to feed from her hands, come like a mystery,
like sunlight rain, a blessing, a bus falling off a bridge,
come like a deserting soldier, a murderer chased by law,
like a girl prostitute escaping her pimp, come like a lost horse,
like a dog dying of thirst, come love, come ragged and melancholy
like the last day on earth, come like a sigh from a sick man,
come like a whisper, like a bump on the road, like a flood,
a dam braking, turbines falling from the sky,
come love like the stench of a swamp, a barrage of light
filling a blind girl's eye, come like a memory
convulsing the body into sobs, like a carcass floating on a stream,
come like a vision, come love like a crushing need,
come like an afterthought. Heart song. Heart song.
The pole smashes and the live wires yellow streaks

on the lush grass. Come look and let me wonder.
Someone. So many. The sounds of footsteps, horses and cars.
Come look and let me wonder. And I stand on my roof
echoing the bird's song and the world says: Do not sleep.
Do not sleep now that you have housed your longing
within the pain of words.

Becoming Kansas

My friend says *yes* to this, *yes* to that,
   Lies in bed all day saying answers,
His life reduced each hour to this: water,

   Paper-thin sheath of flesh, various cancers
That he allows, even befriends.
   Some of us will die of greedier

Diseases, some by their own skeletal hands.
   Others will flicker out; a few will rage.
My friend looks through his window to land

   Draped over itself in green velvet bulges:
Rippling fields, uninterrupted ocean
   From eye to horizon that pulses

With deepening shadow. He used to run
   In those fields. The corn was shoulder high.
Awaiting blindness, he says *yes* again.

   With body inside-out the door's his eye:
Turning to everything, everything enters him.
   So I infect him when he looks at me.

All night he coughs up blood and phlegm.
   The lungs want air, not scenery. Next day,
He sits up in bed and chooses hymns

   For his funeral. If he can stay
Still like this, his body's broken gates
   Unhinged, allowing everything to be

Inside him, saying *yes* to anything that wants
   A body to consume, he thinks
He can become whatever he loves.

   That is why he does not break,
And why the ceaseless answers, always the same.
   And even though tomorrow he will wake

And cough half an hour, expelling his dreams,
   He'll start again, and in fourteen days
He will finish this task. In death, the seam

   Of his body quietly separates,
The word his mouth surrounds now spoken best:
   Eternal, without pitch or beat,

The true music intended when I say *yes*.
   He sings this where we buried him as he
Lets in the winter through his melting breast,
   And Kansas, which he will become, and me.

for Dean Yates (1952–1994)

Woman of Color

The splendid coat that wrapped the favored son
In fevered dreams of adulation
And turned his brothers' hearts from jealousy
To rage (*Behold, this dreamer comes*)—though long
Since rent and soaked in blood, dried and decomposed—
Arrives through the long centuries over
Sea and land, the unexpected birthright
Of this particular girl. Its separate
Magic beads and threads spill onto the floor
Indistinguishable from alphabet
Blocks, the many pieces of her country,
And its citizens loud and teeming from
Their cramped Crayola crayon box. Each state,
Each letter has a color, a shape, its own,
Soft curves and sharp angles, compassionate
Contours promising something not hers to keep,
An abundance utterly unasked for and
Nearly impossible to give. *What is*
This dream that thou hast dreamed? Shall I and thy
Mother and thy brethren indeed come
To bow down ourselves to thee to the earth?

It is loneliness that bows her head, that breaks
Her free from silence's sweet spell, spilling
Her voice onto the brittle air, breathless
In its rush: green of sea, pine, forest, spring;
Blue of midnight, cerulean, cornflower;
Sky, navy, cadet, and royal blue; blue
Violet, turquoise, aquamarine; teal blue,
Blue green, periwinkle; burnt and raw
Sienna, bittersweet, brick and in-
Dian red, goldenrod and thistle, white.

And exile enters here, the lull and pull
Of distance between the voice's deepest source
And its unmappable destinations.
And they sat down to eat bread and they lifted
Up their eyes and looked, and, behold, a company
Of Ishmaelites came from Gilead with
Their camels bearing spicery and balm
And myrrh going to carry it down to
Egypt. And Judah said, What profit is it
If we slay our brother and conceal his blood?
Let us sell him for he is our brother and our flesh.

For her there is no Egypt to seduce
With strange, mad song, no famished countrymen
Falling to their knees and near enough
To make her tremble afraid she will be tender
Instead of stern. Instead there is only
This brilliant coat, a gift of love, that leaves
Her vulnerable to cold and knowing eyes
Until it seems she has no skin at all
Except for silence, except the weave of words:
Hound's tooth, gingham, tulle, eyelet, chambray;
Broadcloth, denim, paisley, linen, wool.
Her dreams grow full of birdsong; each bird says
Its name: Cardinalis Cardinalis,
Anas Carolinensis, Cyanthus
Latirostris, Mimus Polyglottus,
Cyanocitta Stelleri, Agelaius
Phoenecius—over and over,
Until, finally, sure it's meant for her,
She gently stirs the waters' smooth bright skin,
And bursting from the deep into the world,
Its fear, its hurt, its roar; she tries her tongue.

Another Imaginary Voyage

for X—

When cabbalists declare
Each deed we do affects
Beings in other worlds,
My thought turns round to sex,

As it inclines to do,
As needle to true north,
Considering our case,
Weighing it back and forth.

What if we had undressed
That chaste July, and what
If we were being watched
Or watched *for,* as a boat

Reported missing brings
A crowd out to the shore,
To wager whether it
Will or will not appear,

The fog so thick, the sea
Invisible, until
A form coagulates,
And someone calls, "A sail!"

And all things clear. To you,
No comfort; you would see
Yourself step from the deck
Straight into custody;

There follows a swift trial,
A sentence swift and crude
(Reflecting guilt and fear)
To penal servitude.

While I—I can't agree
Touch is a sin, and so
I picture a small crowd
Of sleepless townsfolk who

Have waited out the night
And stand at crimson dawn
Ready to welcome us
With garlands and with wine.

To tell if I am right,
Or you, all books are dumb;
This is among the secrets
Kept by the world to come.

CARL PHILLIPS

The Blue Castrato

I. To His Savior in Christ

If I did not, as I do, know well
to love you first, I'd love my voice
instead, cause you to yield the throne
whose impossibly precious batting I
could sing all day and never start
to know—it is blasphemy or worse
even to think it (*Domine, me—
ut placet—me retine*). I'd love
my voice that is all I need to know
of a clean, a clear, that I am promised
will never leave me, even should
I want it. Who could want it? Even
in this your difficult field, your vale,
I sing—and see? The grasses open.

II. To His Diary

Played Mister Lazy, mostly. Found
the weather fine, but did not step
inside it. Prayed, as usual. Read
the new books that, if I don't watch out,
I shall find myself fairly whelmed
by. Over soup, had wrongful thoughts—
only of wanting something like more
variety, but bad is bad:
said prayer again. Restored, I glued
the handle back on the broken pot
I've never loved: no color, badly
fired. Though it looks more humble now,
I like it more.... The evening quiet.
Some hunger (food, *et al.*). Resisted.

iii. To His Right Hand

Soft!— Is it you? Idiot. Who's
expected? Huh? But his body... I can't
forget it, no. Yes, I can:
don't want to. Still—how easy it is,
remembering, then not, and then
not minding, it's that forgotten. Smell
the bay tree's leaves again, lie down
where it happened, fill the mouth with what
comes closest, the whole time touching
flesh as if flesh were wood, as if luck
could somehow be coaxed from hiding, into
your hand— O dry, and empty. Must
stop wanting. Or less. More sleep. But *how?*,
as usual. I'm better than this. I am.

iv. To His Psychiatrist

Volcano. No, a bud that brooks
no forcing. No. No, now I see
it: my heart. I mean to save it. Here's
Falsetto Childhood; here, bewigged,
is Ardor, antoinetting hot
among a herd that bellows, bleeds.
Here is the pool I spoke of. Dark
is the water, but step up (here, take care)
to the edge: the water clears, is good.
The bulls want only to drink, to cool
what burns, but the water itself is hot.
Steam, then the dream ends. Ends the same:
same fish, marked *help*, swims belly-up
my way. Plays horn. Spits up: —a lily.

v. To His Savior in Christ

Haven't I hymned your praise enough?
What I would not, given the choice, have given,
I gave: my voice is token. For you—
for years, what made for a life—I sang,
I have caused entire crowds to cry
out to you *Uncle;* as pigeons to home,
they sought and came to a kind of resting
upon your deep/your fair/your not-
to-be-understood-in-this-our-life-
time-breast. Forgive me if I say
I'm sometimes sorry. I've licked the broad
tracks that your grace leaves after; sweet?
If I say I've found, known sometimes sweeter,
I'm no less yours. In need, Your Servant.

vi. To His Body at 42 (A Valentine)

Dear Vessel—Little Boat—of Me:
how lovely (still!) you are, resting
on water, you can't know. You know
no field, but drift toward one: there,
each blade of grass wears well its jacket
of dew my Lord Dusk provides—I know,
I tasted, watched each one, formal, bend
then straighten ... years ago. ... Surely
as songdom's Jesus loves you—yes,
I love you too. I wish you sails
of whatever is proof against storm
and what else tears. I wish you fanfare:
cymbals, and flutes; despite a life,
these still-immaculate-sounding notes.

VII. *To His Biographer*

It's true, my star shone anything
but dull—however briefly. For
a time, my voice was such that any
cathedral that I'd sing in—well,
you can still go back and tell the walls
haven't forgotten altogether what
that felt like. Some have said I lacked
passion. It isn't true. I found
that it wasn't enough, moving walls—
can you blame me? Naturally, I quit.
I wanted more. And yes, a part
of that was sex; and part was love . . .
Say I found neither one: I sang,
then didn't. Came, then went away.

VIII. *To His Heirs*

What little of the world I call
(though everything is his, my Lord's,
in the end) my own. My shells, to say
there have been women: Madames Blue,
Consistent, Sorrow, Sorrow's twin . . .
Joy was her name. My furniture.
My wooden fish from Cozumel.
This stone I found there . . . No, he gave
it to me, he for whom the stone
stands against further loss: his hand,
his mouth (*Where are they?*) as he touched
and touched, between his legs, then mine.
Then his, again. Then mine. My soul
to Christ. To you, I these consign.

The White Star

Inside the White Star it was warm, ironed clothes,
and humming revolution of unsteady washer-dryers.
It was whirling blur of red black blue yellow
that Beatrice watched like a TV, next to her lover.

Last night she'd looked into lighted windows
bitterly, as if she'd been evicted, things thrown
out on the sidewalk, cracked lamp, books sprawled
by the mattress, sheaves of paper spilled, all
looking small and naked, exposed, like her once
in a bad dream of childhood.

                    Not yet, except
they'd been kicking some people out on her street,
not her, not yet, not for skin or rent money,
but always perhaps if she forgot to draw her curtains
when she kissed the woman who was not her sister,
when they slow-danced in the kitchen before supper.

Not yet, but already to her. The children taken,
no place of hers, lit or dark, fit for home.

Not yet here to her, but already to a white woman
on the block, standing out by her clothes piled out
to draggle-tail in the dirt, in the getting-dark time,
clouds neon pink, birds going to roost so fast overhead
they left only a single wingbeat in the air.

Already to a brown woman under a mound of blankets
piled by the corner, her head emerging at footsteps,
cautious, fearful, wrinkled turtleneck.
                           Already

to the sallow woman on a laundry bench, wine skin
hot as a blanket, asleep in the clean drunk room.

Tonight in the White Star Muzak was playing old
brittle raindrops. Beatrice leaned sideways against
her lover, smelling her hair and warm clean clothes.
Next bench, a man muttered stones, a woman stared away.

> The padlocked doors, people bending in the rain
> to salvage one obscure object, people shouting
> to no one: *We live here. You can't throw us out.*

She closed her eyes and wished they could dance
in this lit public place. Mouth against the other's ear,
she began to hum: *Go in and out the window, go in
and out.* How the glass would crack under a wrapped fist.
Go in and out the window as we have done before.

HILDA RAZ

Breast/Fever

My new breast is two months old,
gel used in bicycle saddles
for riders on long-distance runs,
stays cold under my skin
when the old breast is warm;
catalogue price, $276. My serial number,
#B-1754, means some sisters under the skin.
My new breast
my new breast is sterile,
will never have cancer.

Once every sixty years
according to the Chinese calendar
comes the year of the golden horse.
Over me your skin is warm,
sweetgel, ribbontongue, goldhorse.
You suck the blank to goose bumps.

HowmIgonnaget there when you're gone
back to your youngthing, sweetcurl?
He moans over your back
twitching your buttons raw. My scar
means nothing to him, a mapletwirl
a whirligig, your center and maypole.

Death waits in the book, the woods,
the TV, the helicopter blades merging
over the house, your hair a fine curl
mist over your haunches, smooth hook near.
You'll curl red over him when I'm under
the ash, gone, all mind or nothing.
Who the hell loves a tree?

Don't tell me on the phone your voice
a fine ringing replica of mine that you've
got sickies, fever, ticks from the job
you won't worry about don't I either
you nut, you bitch dog mother I bred you
out of leaves and mash my blood on the floor
my liver-colored placenta curled in a cold bowl.
Who do you think you are with my sick breasts
on your chest? Oh God let me live to touch her
working out the next generation of women.

Service

I.

Do they hate each other, I wonder,
she who will live on and he who is dying?
I fill their bird feeder with safflower.
Each dip of the orange pitcher scatters seed from its lip
to the earth, in ecstasy. An arc.
A small rain falls down. Bruised light
a nacre over everything.
My breast hurts, shoulder hurts—hurt body—
as I lift my arm to pour, in ecstasy. Alive!
Ready soon to paint their high door.

II.

Perhaps I'm ready to paint the high door.
The phone shrills, four a.m., and I wake
from cicada's trill to cicadas: nothing more.
Far thunder. The rustle the cat makes
reshaping her nest on the floor.
A far train moving cargo.
From the front room, light over the door
where he works all night. Under a microscope once
I watched hooks gouged in paper
by the pen's point, moving,
ink filling in after. A rasp.
And it's morning. Rain.

III.
Car/scars

The car with its pocks and scrapes
offends when God knows what's under his trouser band.
Do they mind skin's markings when what's under works on?
I'm having the door painted.

IV.
The water fit to drink? he asks.
I put up the canning kettle to boil.
She goes to the grocery for distilled water,
maybe listens to the radio en route. Floods.
Thirst, that blessing. I drink and drink from the faucet.
What's under the skin works on in spite of pocks, cut.

V.
En route to the barn, their horses hang their heads over thistles,
for sugar. Girth: barrel-bodies, vats hops-colored, caramel,
the safflower bare-skin scars no trouble to hide.
Are their mouths the width of my hips? Breast? Is their water fit
to drink? They mean no harm
to the world, you say.
Their muzzles are cut-velvet. Apples.

VI.
Fury/night again

Velvet muzzles. They mean no harm
who fit you out. Rain needs the stage now,
chestnuts broadcasting their available stink.
Tuck in your chin, here, sheepskin cup and your tongue cut
on metal, your tongue on sheepskin ... you'll do no harm
to the world. Thirst. No water, fit or no.

VII.
Overheard

Under her skin, poison, but she died well
three years after the doctor said. "I've stopped wondering,"
she said at last, tucking her chin under her teacup.
No nickering. No sugar, no thistles, no apples, no sass,
a pin through her neck. At the fence every day,
you'd never have known her, ribs broken from retching.
Once she was fed earth's bounty.
I'm ready now to paint your high door.

VIII.
My nightshift covers earth's bounty
erased. A shroud would be worse.
No fit water to drink. Blessed thirst.
He writes all night, drags pen
over paper. Light a nacre over everything.
Night. Thistles. Apples. In my palm
velvet muzzle, water. In my breast, a cut mouth.
In my mouth, tongue's cup. High door freshly painted, my arm
lifting in ecstasy, seed pitcher an arc flung high over rain's
ring on the horizon, broken.

Ode (To My Desire)

1
Honey's sweetness thins
in steaming tea;
a drop of honey

thickens to amber
on the pantry counter. Oh,
the sweetening dank, the dark

I inhale: come
on the sheets
on which my lover naps.

A rolled-up paper
uncoils in a whisper:
come is a rose is a star is a monster.

Oh, come all ye faithful,
I sang as a child;
I saw come steam

from every breakfast kettle.
When I was alone,
the day's first come

snaked down the drain. Now
when I dig in the garden,
the come of my forebears

leaks from their coffins.
Come what may,
my love sleeps in a coil.

Come what may, in dreams,
my love spills,
all soul and muscle,

like rows of boys
in high school showers—
how I rode the currents

of that sweet salt river.
"Thy kingdom come,"
I whisper to my lover.

"Thy will be done,"
(half-awake) he sighs.
"Oh, you're a comer,"

I flatter, though
only a little.
"You're a comer," he replies.

2
My love left me
late this morning.
It means nothing.
It means he means
to walk in the foothills,
to take by surprise
a small red bird
in a hackberry.

Then to angle
off-trail—
a narrow canyon—
to a secret rock
beside a pool
(rare this close
to the desert floor).

Spreading a towel,
he will slip
from T-shirt and khakis,
and lie there
on his back, legs
parted slightly,
the sun warming
the surfaces
of his skin,

the skin,
in warming,
growing hazy
and sensitive,
as in a dream.

He knows
(I have told him)
I can go this far.

Then a breeze
along all
the surfaces,

my love dreaming,
naked, of something
in the open air

in a place
he will not
willingly
take me.

The First Woman

She was my Sunday school teacher
when I was just seven and eight.
He was the newly hired pastor,

an albino, alarming sight
with his transparent eyelashes
and mouse-pink skin that looked like it

might hurt whenever she caressed
his arm. Since Eva was her name,
to my child's mind it made great sense

that she should fall in love with him:
He was Adán. Before the Fall
and afterward, her invert twin.

And she, Eva, was blond as well,
though more robust, like Liv Ullmann.
I loved her honey hair, her full

lips; her green eyes a nameless sin.
(Not that I worried all that much—
the church was Presbyterian.)

In Sunday school, her way to teach
us kids to pray was to comment
on all the beauty we could touch

or see in our environment.
My hand was always in the air
to volunteer my sentiment.

Since other kids considered prayer
a chore, the floor was usually mine.
My list of joys left out her hair

but blessed the red hibiscus seen
through the windows while others bowed
their heads. Her heart I schemed to win

with purple prose on meringue clouds.
—For who was Adán, anyway,
I thought, but *nada* spelled backward?

While hers, reversed, called out, *Ave!*
Ave! The lyric of a bird
born and airborne on the same day.

But it was night when I saw her
outside the church for the last time:
yellow light, mosquitoes, summer.

I shaped a barking dog, a fine
but disembodied pair of wings
with my hands. She spoke in hushed tones

with my parents. The next day I would find
myself up north, in a strange house,
without my tongue and almost blind,

there was so much to see. This caused
Cuba, my past, to be eclipsed
in time, but Eva stayed, a loss.

Ave, I learned, meant also this:
Farewell! I haven't seen her since.

Parts of Speech

"Si la uva está hecha de vino, quizá nosotros somos las
palabras que cuentan lo que somos."
—Eduardo Galeano, *El libro de los abrazos*

for Jane Miller

It's the mind that marshals everything into neat sequence
in retrospect—subject, verb, predicate—fooling us
into believing words don't dig their tangled roots in us.
But rooting around we uncover evidence—
fanning files, figures strobe into motion:
In yours, an arm rotates a round stone over a grinding bed;
in mine, hands materialize to tie scalloping vines onto posts.

Behind our names lie the measured crush of grain,
the transliteration of grapes—now abstract, as separate from us
as definitions, definitions that, once removed from the body,
flap like flags claiming the moon. Chances are, our ancestors
were never consumed by dependent or independent clauses
but consumed them instead. Yet what happens to hunger
when what we make is not a thing but an idea, the mind levitating
like a frivolous monarch?

Truth is, the vineyards behind the three-hundred-year-old houses
on the Canary Islands appeared first, wordless,
until, years later, the verb *rodrigar*
jumps out of the *Velázquez* to explain them.
The mind, correcting for the continuity error,
splices it behind the houses, earlier,
so that in the story I tell you I cross the ocean,
verb in hand like a suitcase, ready to lift the vines
into sense, into rows that become the sentences
I am speaking to you—you understand, don't you?—
in a kind of dream, with a fidelity to the future,
spoken by the ventriloquist of the heart.

If you believe the soul is born knowing itself,
then that explains why the famous bullfighter
hides behind his mother's skirts and Churchill stutters as a child,
a record already skipping and popping with age.
And if Julio Cortázar lived life backward—"from cynicism
to innocence, from air to egg"—and Rilke imagines us
"not for a moment hedged by the world of time . . . incessantly
flowing over and over to those who preceded us
and to those who apparently come after us,"
what happens to the grammar that creates us
and whose utterance is apparently dependent on us?

Is this why *Jane* was the first word
I spoke in English, sprawled on the cool tiles of my front porch
in Cuba, a Dick and Jane book spread out before us, my playmates
saying *ha-neh* and I confident about its pronunciation?
The mind, snakily syntactical, places the revelations
in future tense, like that childhood party game
where things are hidden in plain sight: It's the context
that obscures them.

Standing now in what passes for now: the doorway
of my house, night a refectory table between eucalyptus trees—
at its head, in diminishing perspective, the past tense
props elbows on the table like a peasant, ravenous.
Closer there gleams a skyline of covered dishes.
Here come the subverting voles of volition,
the picnic ants of anticipation.

Notes:
    The idea that the soul is born knowing itself comes from Jungian psychologist James Hillman, who uses the examples of the bullfighter and Churchill to illustrate his point.
    Quote about Cortázar is from his friend Eduardo Galeano.
    The Rilke quote comes from a 1925 letter to his Polish translator regarding explication of Sonnets to Orpheus.

The Mistaken Nymph

It was only the marvelous gravity of your attention,
That weighed me down, that made me seem self-delighted,
Sunk like the moon in a mandarin's cup of reflections,
But truly I was suggestible as the morning.
When you laced wings on your shoulders, birds rippled over
My smile; when you hunted and crimsoned
Into a spear, I bristled, displayed, muttered *British*.
You loved me for nothing I was but your faultless recording.

O Echo, synecdoche of a forest of sorrows,
It wasn't a copy-book passion: my element always
Charged you with something its own, but my bravest flights
You tore from the sky and clamped to my wrists labeled Crime.
Now slumped in my mud, I ask why
Could I not have been born that irresistible flower-boy,
His slashed jeans saggy and plump in all the right places,
And you on your tiptoes, begging to dive, O.K.,
To die, in the dried-up honey-pot of his addiction.

In the part of my brain that's deep as a dressing table,
I've kept every look you gave me, magenta to moonstone.
I don't need a pool or a glass,
I know how I've changed—only men are surprised by their faces:
It's as if my blood had been dragged from me, pocket by pocket
Found guilty in some dead airport room, the whiteness
Stitched in my bra, declared on my lips. Call it terror.
Yours or mine, I've slept with my life pressed against it.

GRACE SCHULMAN

Elegy Written in the Conservatory Garden

In memoriam: Irving Howe

Hearing the news, we headed for this garden,
a children's picture book, a black-and-white
movie turned to color for the Oz scenes.

We'd planned to take him here. In this arbor,
crabapple trees enclose us like a vault,
their branches splayed like nerve ends over us.

It is before the soul has slipped from the body.
He is the blurred form moving through warped trees
like fingers on a harp. I say at last,

"In summer when we walked in the meadow
he swore the lilacs spurred him more than quarrels."
(Later, I read he'd whispered to a friend,

"In Paris once, alone on a stone bench
between rose shrubs, I knew
that death, if it meant coming into that,

might be all right.") But even now,
I know he's here, behind a screen of roses,
fragrant, pink-to-golden in the sun—

but not the man you knew, who claimed
you missed the real stuff of a Beckett play.
You listen, fidget, and turn to the park's edge,

where towers poke out of elms the park's designers
hoped would hide the city's pipes, and squint
at an ornate eight-sided loggia

stuck like a Renaissance scholar's cap
on the hospital where you tend the sick,
and where you left him alive hours ago.

You don't know why he died so suddenly.
For you, true faith is evidence. And now,
your hands sort twigs to brace a fallen aster:

they are splinting a child's arm.
I say, "This garden may be paradise—"
and hesitate. This is too soiled for heaven,

too various: nasturtiums shine, their odor
of cocoa-mulch merges with hints of urine;
spray paint adorns wisteria arbor walls;

a sea-blue bottle lies smashed on the walk;
boys in grimy shirts sketch daffodils.
On asphalt, blossoms blend with candy wrappers,

or lie in grooves, white yellowing like newsprint,
under a bench splattered with pigeon droppings
where we have lunch, saving our soda cans

for a man who spears them from the trash.
Look: by our feet, a toddler rips out a rose.
We do not move to stop her. It is her angel.

We haven't said his name. A handbill tells us
crocuses and lilies store food underground—
just where we store his rimless glasses.

Now, flicking a petal from your shoulder,
you say, "We'll see the spirea last
through summer, and turn golden in the autumn."

I shudder at the word autumn.
I've read cycads grew with dinosaurs
and stood with Adam in the Garden of Eden.

We rise, as though to visit him again,
and touch a magnolia tree that may live forever,
always, with our thumbprints on its trunk.

When I Was White

When I was white I came and went, a cycle
of blood and moon and tide, hid nothing
of gun-shape inside me, debated evil

with no one. I said: Bring me something
handsome to eat and they did, that steak butter,
you could spread it on bread. I said: Bring

me taxis. They flew to my side and uttered
Get in and *Where to,* just the thing to carry me.
I said: We are all the same No Matter

What. This was my zaniest folly.
I had blinders on the sides of my head
big as real estate, blue as jelly. We

are all the same Underneath, I said,
and you could count the dusty liberals
nodding in deadly agreement, dead

as the Pope, dead as the Nazis, doornail
dead like the sunnies along Lake Michigan
and the poor bastard steadying his pole

ten feet up the beach. Jesus again,
this time with a sweet brown Chuckie B. face,
and I am beside you in the Bargain

Villa on Clark. I've traveled decades
through dead seas, I've seen my people flap
on their sides as they die of too much shade,

you can count them piling up on the maps
of the world, the unsightly word *equal*
a sticky drool from the Oh of their lips.

Blue

See my colors fall apart? Green
to yellow with just one shade gone,
the changing tints of your sun-struck eyes,
if there were sun. Today the prism held to mine's

a prison, locking in the light. In one of those mirrors
the colors are true. In one of these pictures the pigment's
my own. The sound there is aquarelle and indigo,
and dripping distant water, the day's habitual failure

to be anything substantial. Today a blank like color
by numbers, filled in with fog that frames the lake
in transient tones. That's the color I mean, some mist
painting the shore pastel and pointillist

rain, painting the shadow between window and light. Today
each hue dissolves in humid air, transparency
I try to grasp and then let go, clear overflow
of waves on gravel. The mist with its single-dipped brush

smears itself across the canvas of the pines.
The pines, knowing no better, run together on a morning
palette. Today the scene's dismantled, that can't be
dismissed. *I once was blind, but now*

I see my landscape attenuate itself, drowned lake
of evergreens. On a morning like this with new crayons
I drew a man, that red valentine
in the side. The picture of two hands scrawling the outline

where only one thing's missing; the crayons scattering
from childish fingers. Color me or leave me vacant.

EDMUND WHITE

The Tea Ceremony

from *The Farewell Symphony*

Tomorrow is Toussaint in Paris, All Saint's Day, and I suppose I'll visit Brice's little white marble plaque in the columbarium at Père Lachaise. Why do I avoid it for months on end?

I keep thinking of a couple of Americans we met during the year before Brice died. One of them, Thomas, was a heavy, stoop-shouldered man like me, and like me he had a barrel chest that descended directly into a barrel waist. Unlike me he still wore a mustache, which was gray and so thick it covered his upper lip. His hair he treated like an accessory he despised and he batted at it with his hand or slapped it impatiently away from his brow.

His lover, Giles Satsumi, was a Japanese-American lawyer in his thirties who no longer practiced. He'd been brought up in San Francisco and had known two of my friends who'd migrated there from New York in the early eighties and died in the first three years of the plague. Giles was always smiling and knew all the lyrics to Noel Coward's and Cole Porter's songs. He kept nodding other people into agreement. He never spoke about himself and seemed more intent on understanding whatever was light and amusing about his guests than in confiding his darker secrets or eliciting theirs.

Tom was from an old New England family that had made a small but necessary military item. He apparently had a large enough fortune to finance a life of decorous leisure. But, since they were Americans, Tom and Giles felt the need to improve themselves even if in rather disjointed and ultimately useless ways. They studied cooking at the Cordon Bleu in Paris. They'd toured gardens as far apart as Vancouver, Sissinghurst, Nara, and Florence. Giles had also spent months in Japan learning the tea ceremony and buying fabulously expensive cracked and mended pots and exquisitely crude Korean cups. They'd purchased a little house in the eighth arrondissement in Paris that for them was just a bagatelle, since they rarely lived there.

"It's so funny," Giles said in his choppy, rat-a-tat way that made everyone laugh but that did not coerce laugher, "we're so naïve, Tom and I, at least about certain things, that when we bought this house we couldn't fathom why any residence would have eight bedrooms, each with a *bidet,* and no kitchen, until our French friends, stifling their *éclats de rire,* explained to us we'd just bought a bordello!" That one French expression, with its double *r,* so tricky for American uvulas, was so perfectly produced that I remembered they'd also studied French diction with a private instructor.

In honor of this *bonbonnière* from the turn of the century with its fake Greek statues of laughing girls in shorty peplums and slipping togas, its slender Ionic columns in the tiny salon that appeared to be made of lightly licked spun sugar, and its court-yard fountain of a verdigrised Pan leering over his pipes while a drunken naiad embraced his hooves, Tom and Giles had covered their windows with crackling yellow satin curtains and their Louis XVI *bergères* with a faded lemony and beige tapestry. Every-thing looked as though it had just been pulled out of a dress shop box and flung with prodigal abandon over a bed. I could imagine a cocotte in an ice-blue peignoir trimmed in coffee lace smoking a cigarette in the salon and listening to a wind-up Victrola play-ing a recording of Mistinguette. The bathroom upstairs was royal, intended more for the piquant display of pink female flesh to spe-cial customers than for routine hygiene.

We ate a "gourmet" dinner and I remembered to keep up a constant stream of *ooh*s and *ah*s and compliments, which sound-ed so exaggerated to Brice that he raised an eyebrow and suspect-ed me of mockery until I explained to him later that Americans don't mock each other, at least not with such subtle cruelty, and that among Americans praise any less dithyrambic would have struck our host as poorly concealed disappointment.

After dinner, Giles asked if we'd like to participate in a tea cere-mony. Brice had just recovered from a bout of wasting brought on by a bacterium in the blood related to tuberculosis and though his cure was miraculous he was still thin and weak.

"How long does it last?" I asked.

"About an hour."

"And we're seated cross-legged on tatami mats the whole time?"

"On tatami, but most Westerners lounge about or even lie down."

"But I want to do it," Brice said. "I'm sure it's very spiritual and beautiful." The problem with dying for an atheist is that there are no normal spiritual occasions; exotic ones—or improvised moments—are made to bear a heavy weight.

Giles nodded and left the room. Tom woof-woofed a bit like a faithful family dog. He was companionable and heartbreakingly kind but he seemed a bit lost without his brilliant companion, so decisive, so magnetic, so full of amusing ideas.

After ten minutes Tom led us into the courtyard, where we were supposed to remain silent and drink sips of water from the fountain (this absurd fountain of lean, leering Pan and lubricious maiden). Tom said, "We're purifying ourselves from the dust of the outside world. Our thoughts must settle." I worried that Brice, so fragile and bony, might catch cold despite his many layers of shirts, sweaters, and vests, but I could see he was concentrating and participating in everything with great seriousness.

We went into a narrow but high room (one of the many *chambres d'assignation*?) that was carpeted with tatami on platforms around a recessed fire and bubbling cauldron of hot water. Giles was outfitted in elaborate robes of many layers, the outermost of black silk. His shoulders were motionless somewhere under the stiff peaks. Wearing a glossy round black hat and a sort of brocaded apron, he seemed a cross between a Shinto priest and a Masonic Grand Master. He was easygoing and quick to explain things and laughed at passing awkwardnesses, but nevertheless the room, the costume, and the singing of the kettle made him seem more subdued.

Brice was panting slightly, no doubt from the pain of sitting on his uncushioned bones, those hipbones that looked as huge as an old nag's when he was naked and the bulb at the base of his spine where the coccyx had worn red and become inflamed. But his eyes were sparkling with the excitement.

Tom, in stocking feet and trousers, big belly hanging over his belt, scooted about on his knees, the grave, mustachioed acolyte serving the young priest and presenting us, the communicants, first with small, beautiful, and nearly tasteless rice cakes and, after the elaborate brewing and whisking, the foamy, bitter green tea. Giles explained everything he was doing. He showed us the ancient elements of the tea service. He explained the painting on the wall. He demonstrated the method for receiving the cup and turning it a hundred and eighty degrees away in order to drink modestly from the inferior side and to present the superior side, with a bow, to the next drinker. We examined the black lacquered caddy and the bright green dry tea piled high inside it to resemble Mt. Fuji. After two rounds of tea the bowls were rinsed and dried with a smart swipe of a folded towel. "Now you're allowed to handle the bowls and look at them from every angle, since often a visitor might see a particular bowl only once in his lifetime." I could see that Brice was sweating from the effort to stay seated this way but that he was charmed by such a fussy ritual combining spirituality and connoisseurship.

Nine months later, on New Year's, just three months before Brice was to die, we were invited back, this time with Brice's brother Michel, a big, strapping weight lifter from Nice who, despite his bulging muscles, was every bit as much an aesthete as Brice himself. Since he was shy and in any event spoke no English, he was very quiet, but he, too, marveled at the refinement of the ceremony, conducted so improbably in this Belle Epoque *maison de passe.* The elements of the tea service were all decorated this time with silver and gold, since these precious metals were considered to bring good luck, appropriate to a New Year's tea. Giles was extremely attentive to Brice, who was now ectoplasmically thin; his cheekbones looked as though they'd burst through the translucent yellow parchment of his skin. And yet Giles was driven to complete this dolorous if inspiring ritual in the most exacting manner.

Brice died and I received a condolence note from Giles and Tom. Six months later, Tom sent me a black-bordered printed Bristol announcing Giles's death. I called our only mutual friend, who told me that Giles had been ill for years, but able to travel, cook, garden, make tea. When his health suddenly took a turn for the worse at the end of the summer, he'd refused all medication and faded in two weeks. Tom, his passionately devoted lover, had vanished, inconsolable. No one knew where he was. It seemed strange to me that Giles had never spoken of his own status and that of the five participants in the New Year's Day tea, two were dead.

ABOUT MARILYN HACKER

A Profile by Rafael Campo

Award-winning poet and renowned editor, lesbian activist and literary formalist, native New Yorker and expatriate American in Paris—Marilyn Hacker, who is all these identities and more, gloriously defies all attempts at easy categorization. "It's not a question of an issue," she says in describing the relationship between her art and her convictions, "but a question of the people I know who are close to me, who are health-care workers or living with illnesses, or the neighbors, housed and homeless, I pass on the street, or the grocery store that goes out of business where I've bought my salad and broccoli every day for the past five years. All of those may be reflected or transformed in my work."

Marilyn Hacker was born in 1942 and raised in the Bronx, the only child of working-class Jews who were the first in their respective families to go to university. Her mother had earned a master's degree in chemistry, which, according to Hacker, "entitled her to work as a saleswoman at Macy's." It was the midst of the Great Depression, and jobs were scarce. Even as the economy improved, opportunities could still be limited. "She was told she couldn't go to medical school because she was a woman and a Jew. So she became a teacher in the New York City public school system." Meanwhile, Hacker's father was only occasionally employed as an industrial chemist, leaving her mother with the responsibilities of the breadwinner; after finally finding professional satisfaction as a teacher at City College, he died of pancreatic cancer at the age of forty-eight.

Despite the many difficulties and discouragements her parents faced, Hacker enthusiastically took on academic challenges. Her formidable intellect propelled her through the prestigious Bronx High School of Science, and she skipped her senior year. She enrolled at New York University at the age of fifteen. She says of her own precocity, "I wouldn't recommend that anyone go to university at fifteen. It really is like giving a fifty-dollar bill to a child and turning her loose in a Godiva chocolate shop." Existentialism and French literature competed with calculus for her attentions, and she read widely and voraciously.

With one year left before graduation, Hacker married her high school alter ego, science fiction writer Samuel Delany, and they settled in New York's East Village. She had fallen in love with writing, and a writer. "I worked at all kinds of jobs, mostly commercial editing," she recalls. Eventually, she returned to NYU, edited the university literary magazine, publishing poems by Charles Simic and Grace Schulman, and graduated with a bachelor of arts degree in Romance languages. In the next decade, she and Delany (soon separated) would both become known as outspoken queer writers.

Informed by the rigorous science courses she had tackled in NYU's laboratories, and yet peopled by the rebellious and flamboyant characters she encountered in the corner bars and pool halls of her neighborhood, Hacker's poetry began to flourish. "I started to send my work to journals when I was twenty-six, which was just a question of when I got the courage up," she says. Always a passionate reader and supporter of literary magazines, she quickly adds, "They were mostly journals I had been reading for the previous six or seven years." Her first publication was in Cornell University's venerable *Epoch*. After moving to London in 1970, she found a transatlantic audience through the pages of *The London Magazine* and *Ambit*. Her greatest breakthrough came when Richard Howard, then editor of *The New American Review*, accepted three poems for publication. The excitement still bubbling in her voice, she remembers, "I didn't know him, I'd never met him, nobody or nothing in common except that I loved his work, and I got a transatlantic letter saying not only thank you for sending these poems, I'm taking three, but also, are there more?"

She did have more. When she was thirty-one, with her new mentor having helped her circulate a manuscript, *Presentation Piece* was published by the Viking Press. The response to the work was electric: the book, a Lamont Poetry Selection of the Academy of American Poets, also received a National Book Award. Since then, she has published seven additional volumes, culminating last year in the release of both *Winter Numbers* and her *Selected*

PHOTO: ROBERT GIARD

Poems: 1965–1990 from W.W. Norton. She continues to attract prizes: most recently, *Winter Numbers* garnered a Lambda Literary Award and *The Nation*'s Lenore Marshall Prize, and her *Selected Poems* received the 1996 Poets' Prize.

Such success has not come without a price. *Winter Numbers* details her experience of the loss of many friends to AIDS and breast cancer, and her own struggle with the latter epidemic. Months after she completed chemotherapy, she lost her influential job as editor of *The Kenyon Review,* after a four-year tenure whose tremendous impact on the literary landscape is still being felt. She says of her time there, when she joined the emerging voices of gays and lesbians, women, and people of color to those of the country's literary elect, "We sometimes received—and I would read—two hundred manuscripts a week. Some of them were wonderful, some were terrible; most were mediocre. It was like the gifts of the good and bad fairies. There were rich rewards that came to me: discovering new writers like Aleida Rodríguez, Rane Arroyo, and Carl Phillips. And there were established writers whom I came to know through working with them, like Herbert Blau, Adrienne Kennedy, and Hayden Carruth."

Hacker acknowledges that there is some tension between her

own writing and the editing work through which she has also distinguished herself. "For me, editing can be frustrating, but invigorating—something I love to do. Until I was editor of *The Kenyon Review,* it was mostly something I did without pay, a habit I had to feed by doing other work. When I edited *Thirteenth Moon,* a feminist literary magazine (now at SUNY Albany), I basically supported it myself with an essential grant here and there... There can be a conflict, because of the constant influx of other writers' words and preoccupations." Still, she has consistently managed to do both, serving also as editor of *The Little Magazine,* the science fiction magazine *Quark,* and as a guest editor once before of *Ploughshares.* When asked directly about the impact of her own editing work, she modestly deflects the question towards encouraging young writers to read more of the literary magazines to which they often send their work. "I've been an inveterate reader of literary magazines since I was a teenager. There are always discoveries. You're sitting in your easy chair, reading; you realize you've read a story or a group of poems four times, and you know, Yes, I want to go farther with this writer."

Just as she avoids crediting herself for the mark she has made as an editor, Hacker is reluctant to accept what might be called the healing power of her poetry, which has been a source of inspiration to many struggling with their own experiences of illness. "I don't think that's something a writer can claim without a sort of hubris. I have experienced healing through other writers' poetry, but there's no way I can sit down to write in the hope a poem will have healing potential. If I do, I'll write a bad poem." However, she does recognize the importance of the imagination and self-expression in dealing with suffering. "Another artist's perceptions can incite your own. Last week, I was visiting an extraordinary young woman writer and critic who is HIV-positive and in the hospital with PCP and suspected TB. I noticed *The Magic Mountain* by Thomas Mann atop all the other books on her shelf. I can see why it was there."

Given the immediacy of the themes in her work, it is understandable that Hacker has little patience for those who would make an issue of differences between so-called "formal poetry" and free verse. She puts it bluntly: "I think it's a non-issue. There are other struggles in which I would much rather be engaged." Of her own affinity for received forms, she blithely says, "It's not a statement of my politics or an aesthetic I'd impose...it's purely hedonistic." The books on her own bedside table reflect more her concerns as a writer and activist than her prosodic mastery, from Lucy Grealy's *Autobiography of a Face* and the biography of Paul Celan, *Poet Survivor Jew*, to Julia Alvarez's *The Other Side* and Mark Doty's *Atlantis*.

Marilyn Hacker lives in Paris and in Manhattan, with her life partner of ten years, physician assistant Karyn London. Wake Forest University Press will soon publish *Edge*, her translations of the French poet Claire Malroux. She will teach at Brandeis this fall and at Princeton next spring. Her words about this issue of *Ploughshares* epitomize what she herself stands for, and what she will continue to do for many years to come: "Good writing gives energy, whatever it is about. But the fact that writers are dealing with essential issues, that some are themselves implicated as HIV-positive or writing with cancer or AIDS, or as health-care givers, legal advisors, teachers, outreach workers, witnesses—I think that's a necessary integration of literary writing with what's actually going on in our world."

Rafael Campo's work appears in this issue of Ploughshares *and* Best American Poetry 1995, *and is also forthcoming in* Parnassus *and the AIDS-related poetry anthology* Things Shaped in Passing: Poets for Life II, *due out from Persea Books this spring. Marilyn Hacker, while at* The Kenyon Review, *was the first editor to publish his work.*

THE CHAIN *Poems by Tom Sleigh. Univ. of Chicago Press, $35.00 cloth, $11.95 paper. Reviewed by H. L. Hix.*

Tom Sleigh's third collection, *The Chain*, reads as if the history of poetry culminated in his voice. From the beginning, Sleigh's book encompasses, and is encompassed by, the mythical. "Lamentation on Ur," an "adaptation, from a French version, of a Babylonian original," reminds the reader that the ancient need not be *made* modern, but always is so already. Subtitled "2,000 B.C.," the poem mirrors ourselves at 2,000 A.D., and thrives, as every myth must, on music, music, music. "Our country's dead / melt into the earth," it tells us, but listen to Sleigh as he sings their dirge: they are "annihilated / / by the double-bladed axe. Heavy, beyond / help, they lie still as a gazelle / exhausted in a trap, / muzzle in the dust." Such deft alliteration and internal rhyme might make Sleigh seem a light-handed Hopkins or young Yeats, and a match for a maestro like Robert Bringhurst, to whose "The Petelia Tablet" Sleigh's poem is sister.

But *The Chain* embodies more than myth; its ontogeny recapitulates the phylogeny of lyric as well. If Petrarch does not lurk nor Shakespeare speak in "The Work," that sonnet sequence shows Sleigh has spent time at their knees. Even as his father is "poured out" into "darkness unquenchably long," Sleigh gives him life, "So that even as he hurtles he keeps holding / / Back like a dam the flood overtops." His father's "body's fevered presence / Shimmers like the phantom heat that will trail / Up the pipe of the crematory oven." The father becomes, inevitably, both effigy and Ephialtes: the sonnet identified as a dream ends, "Face wholly unwoven, without heart, mind, you / Are nothing in my hands but my hands moving."

Our more proximate heritage also inhabits these poems. Phrases from the modern masters are hidden in the poems like lockets of a lover's hair: "loops and whorls" finds its way from Roethke's greenhouse to the fingerprints of Sleigh's incarcerated character in "The Tank," and "fixed stars govern a life" moves from Plath's "Words" to the "Epilogue" of Sleigh's "Terminus." But their voices also resonate in other ways, as in the rhythms of Sleigh's villanelle "The Explanation," which, "Sifting like a lover unspoken promises and explanations," favors all its aunts and uncles: Roethke and Plath, Empson and Thomas, Bishop and Bidart.

All this would be insult, though, an assertion of derivativeness, did not Sleigh's book infuse the mythical, the lyric, and the modern with the personal. George Oppen was right to observe that "what one must add to the tradition is conviction. One's own." Like the subject in his "Crossing the Border," Sleigh "realizes that the old formulas are useless here" until one arrives at "the limits of the known world." For Sleigh, "It's as if the world below demanded / A way of speaking never dreamt of— / / That circles invisibly as radar / Registering the slightest flicker in the soul." These poems are, as Socrates says beauty always will be, liberated and liberating. To the singer of these poems, his own final words apply: "even as its wings begin to beat, / His soul's eyes peer into his face."

H. L. Hix's most recent book is Spirits Hovering Over the Ashes: Legacies of Postmodern Theory *(SUNY Press, 1995). His first book of poems,* Perfect Hell, *recently won the Peregrine Smith Poetry Award and will be published this year by Gibbs Smith.*

YOU HAVE THE WRONG MAN *Stories by Maria Flook. Pantheon Books, $22.00 cloth. Reviewed by Fred Leebron.*

First as a poet, and then as a novelist, Maria Flook has established herself as a writer with an astonishing vision—an artist who refuses to blink. Now, in her first book of stories, *You Have the Wrong Man,* Flook continues to mine, with richness and sophistication, the difficult lives of desperate people. These eight complex and relentless stories chronicle men and women who quixotically, perpetually embrace wrong lovers and company. The language is as hard and sharp as the lives the stories reveal, and yet the book is rooted in elegance and surprising humor.

In "Lane," an ambivalent medical student analyzes his lengthy crush on a calculating but naïve college classmate who has since become a bestselling novelist. He's the wrong man for Lane, she's the wrong woman for him, and their relationship is rife with squirming misfortune: he suffers from a disfiguring scar that virtually "halves" his face; she earns a black eye in a bar fight; his right hand endures one of the most excruciating minutes of fiction squashed within a window; and ultimately she dissolves his amorous intentions by opening her gown to reveal "a tiny oblong sore spoiling the silky vestibule below her clitoris." "I have learned to embrace the grimy little mysteries I come across," the medical student notes at one point, "giving full rein to my sense of humor."

All of the major players in this collection are scarred and yet remain "still in harm's way." "Prince of Motown" is the ultimate wrong man story. Rick's mother is an assistant director at a shelter for battered and abused women, where Iris, a teenage mother of a sickly infant, seeks refuge. She hasn't been beaten by her boyfriend, but by the boyfriend's *aunt,* who swats the girl with a box of Reynolds Wrap, "sawing its serrated edge across Iris's face... She tried to protect herself but Estelle sawed the box across Iris's tight jawbone. The strip of metal teeth was sharp and left deep cuts. Dots of blood lifted in two intersecting ellipses lines. Iris wiped her chin and blood came off on the palm of her hand. 'You cut me! You cut me!' " The older women at the shelter match Iris wound for wound as they exchange war stories one morning, delivering a riveting catalog of abuse, but emotionally, Iris is already "many dangerous miles ahead." She has little choice but to return to the household of her baby's father, his mother, and his aunt.

These stories are remarkably honest, and their language is as clean and brilliant as something scrubbed and polished. The transvestite in "Exchange Street" knows that her boyfriend wants "to enter her where her stitches tugged her sphincter together like a sausage casing. Venice told him, 'I'm probably going to faint, you understand?' " In "Rhode Island Fish Company," the scarred tattoo on the narrator's niece's arm looks like "the fell on a leg of lamb, the blotted violet ink of a meat inspector's stamp beneath a yellow scab the size of a wallet," and the niece's hair dressing smells "peculiarly familiar, like diaphragm jelly." The sexual attraction the narrator feels for her niece's boyfriend is "the current of heat that flows upward from the pelvis to the brain in an instant recognition. I felt its flashpowder aftertaste in the back of my throat."

Throughout *You Have the Wrong Man,* Flook evocatively and intelligently portrays men and women confronting their despera-tion, while trying to keep intact that narrow and vital strip of energy with which they were born. Poetic in language and novel-istic in scope, these stories unveil new truths with an unerring and compassionate voice.

Fred Leebron's first novel, Out West, *will be published by Doubleday this year. He is also co-editor of the forthcoming* Postmodern American Fiction: A Norton Anthology.

ATLANTIS *and* HEAVEN'S COAST *Poems and a memoir by Mark Doty. HarperCollins, $12.00 paper and $23.00 cloth. Reviewed by Diann Blakely Shoaf.*

Mark Doty's third collection, *My Alexandria,* won the 1993 National Book Critics Circle Award, and his new volume of poems, *Atlantis,* crowns its predecessor's substantial achieve-ments. Its mythical title notwithstanding, the realm of *Atlantis* is fully human, subject to forces that make most things seem "fallen down, broken apart, carried away." Yet among Doty's notable strengths is his ability to celebrate this realm of grief and loss as a place that nonetheless offers an array of "gorgeous[ness]."

For instance, in "Crepe de Chine," a poem that resonates with both splendor and trash, a drag queen, walking along a Manhattan avenue, becomes intoxicated by shop windows filled with giant bottles of perfume, then by the various glassed displays of pastries and flowers: "I want to wear it," the speaker says of this lavish ex-cess, "I want to put the whole big thing / on my head, I want . . . / / [to] take the little florists' shops / and twist them into something / for my hair, forced spiky branches / and a thousand tulips." In a world where signs of wreckage stain and fade a land-scape increasingly depopulated by plague, and where so much is beyond our control, the conclusion's campy defiance reverberates like a horn blown in a Renaissance court: "look at me built and re-built, / / torn down to make way, / excavated, trumped up, tricked out, / done, darling, / / in every sense of the word. Now, / you call me / Evening in Paris, call me Shalimar, / call me Crepe de Chine."

Doty's attentive eye is equally at home in the natural world; indeed, while in poems like "Crepe de Chine" and "Two Cities" he seems guided by the Elizabethan-drenched and urban soul of Hart Crane, in others he seems led by Elizabeth Bishop, perhaps the best observer of the Atlantic coast's various forms of cold, clear knowledge. "At the Boatyard" even features the appearance of a "whiskered, placid" seal, an homage to Bishop's twin and totem in "At the Fishhouses." For Bishop and Doty, description is an ethos as well as an aesthetic, commanding us to honor otherness by lending it our full sensuous and "self-forgetful" concentration, as Bishop wrote of Darwin, before we begin to form conceptions. Perception and conception, nature and city, flower and frost—all these supposed opposites come together in the rich fusion and profusion of "Grosse Fuge." Written after Cape Cod was visited in rapid succession by Hurricane Bob and a false spring, the poem contrapuntally weaves the storm's aftermath, a friend's temporary recovery from AIDS-related dementia, and the experiencing of Beethoven's late quartets. "What can you expect, in a world that blooms / and freezes all at once?" Doty asks at the end of the poem. The answer lies in the musical form itself, "this stream of theme and reiteration, statement / and return" which closes with no great pronouncement, simply a reckoning: "There is no resolution in the fugue."

A partner's death from AIDS is the core of the six-poem sequence that gives *Atlantis* its title, and the core as well of Doty's just-released prose memoir, *Heaven's Coast*. Its lyrical treatment of time, as well as the attention paid to the various chapters' natural or urban settings—Cape Cod, Boston, New York, Vermont—link the memoir to *Atlantis* in ways both frictive and enriching.

The affirmative notes struck in "Crepe de Chine"—"look at me built and rebuilt"—echo beneath the multiple and overlapping stories of loss in *Heaven's Coast*, but in the memoir these notes occur polyphonically rather than arising from a solo. For *Heaven's Coast* isn't only Doty's story; it's the story of AIDS and the ravenous swath it has cut through his—and our—community. Against the disease's hideous gaping hunger, Doty posits the imperfect but healing construct of friendship, the families we choose and make and remake and also find ourselves remade by.

"It's the drag queen's perennial message, after all," Doty says in one of the memoir's final chapters: *"we're all self-made here."*

Diann Blakely Shoaf is a regular reviewer for the "Bookshelf." Her collection of poems, Hurricane Walk, *was published by BOA Editions in 1992.*

EMERALD CITY *Stories by Jennifer Egan. Nan A. Talese/Doubleday. $22.50 cloth. Reviewed by Jodee Stanley.*

In the title story of Jennifer Egan's collection, *Emerald City,* a young photographer's assistant walks down the streets of Manhattan with his girlfriend, an unsuccessful model. He takes in the street noise, the dark storefronts, looking for something that will ground him in this scene, which is at once familiar and elusive. Then, when he catches their reflection in a windowpane, it strikes him "that this was New York: a place that glittered from a distance even when you reached it."

In this and other stories, Egan writes with glorious clarity about people seeking to transcend their present situations; in the end, however, they tend to arrive at places that are more imagined than real, their longing revealed as naïveté or nostalgia. In "Sacred Heart," a Catholic school student envisions the "dark and troubled life" of a classmate who has run away from home. When she finds her friend downtown, working in a discount shoestore, she is dismayed: "I still clung to the vague belief that she had risen above the earth and now lived among those fat, silvery clouds I'd seen from airplane windows. What I felt, seeing her, was a jolt of disappointment."

Several of the stories are set in foreign locales, while others take place in more familiar settings: San Francisco, suburban Illinois. Whether the backdrop is exotic or humble, Egan uses her extraordinary craft to bring the reader into the intimate landscape of her characters—both the physical and psychological worlds in which they live. In "Puerto Vallarta," a young girl who has discovered her father's infidelity searches for a way to recover her respect for him on a family vacation to Mexico. In "The Watch Trick," a casual boat ride on Lake Michigan ends in a scuffle between old friends, when jealousies surface and a past betrayal is revealed. And in the brilliant story "Why China?" a businessman takes his family to the Xi'an province as he tries to distance himself from allegations of fraud back in the U.S. Traveling through the alien and enchanting Chinese countryside, he confronts the hollowness of the affluent life he has created, and the uncertainty of what will follow as it crumbles. "The land got very strange. Gray hills bulged from the earth in such a way that their middles looked wider than their bases.... I stared out the window at the weird hills and told myself that we lived in San Francisco, in a house on Washington Street that I'd bought for a million in cash six years ago, that our house existed right now, the burglar alarm on, automatic sprinklers set to keep the garden alive. It's all still there, I thought. Waiting. But I didn't believe it."

In her acclaimed debut novel *The Invisible Circus,* Egan demonstrated her talent for storytelling with remarkably fluid and assured prose. In *Emerald City,* she reaches beyond her first book, giving us stories that don't simply ring with truth, but shimmer with it. All the characters in her collection look for a moment when everything will come together—the last, mysterious piece of the puzzle—and of course, most are heartbroken. But others briefly, tantalizingly peek at perfection, "and for a moment the world ignites, it blazes around them with exquisite radiance. Each detail is right."

≈

*Books Recommended by
Our Advisory Editors*

Andre Dubus recommends *Women in Their Beds,* stories by Gina Berriault: "For decades Gina Berriault has been a hidden treasure. Now we have thirty-five of her stories in one book. Buy it, and don't lend it to anyone. Her work keeps going out of print." (Counterpoint)

Maxine Kumin recommends *Old Mother, Little Cat: A Writer's Reflections on Her Kitten, Her Aged Mother,* *and ... Life,* a memoir by Merrill Joan Gerber: "This is a deeply affecting book, told absolutely without artifice; unflinching but compassionate, and very charming. Gerber is best known as a novelist and short story writer. She was the darling of *The New Yorker* in the sixties. This is a new voice for her." (Longstreet)

Don Lee recommends *Take Three,* poems by Thomas Sayers Ellis, Joe Osterhaus, and Larissa Szporluk: "An innovative and worthy new annual series from Graywolf, edited by *Agni*'s Askold Melnyczuk. Designed to launch the work of new poets, this first volume presents about twenty-five poems by each of these young writers—three very different, vibrant voices that deserve attention and appreciation." (Graywolf)

Philip Levine recommends *The Mortal City,* translations by William Matthews of one hundred epigrams by the Latin poet Martial: "The best book of translations I've read in ages. Matthews manages to make a first-century A.D. poet who wrote in Latin sound both like a Roman and a contemporary. All the wit you find in Matthews's own work, the intelligence, the daring, quick moves, are here. Matthews, who can think inside a poem better than anyone else I know of writing in English today, shows us one of the great sources of his inspiration. The book is brilliantly and economically introduced. A collection to be read, reread, and cherished." (Ohio Review Books)

James Alan McPherson recommends *Blues and Trouble,* short stories by Tom Piazzi: "In these stories, Tom Piazzi is touching the grain of actual, as opposed to imaginary, human life. He sees both the pain and the humor, the tragic as well as the comic." (St. Martin's)

Joyce Peseroff recommends *Girl Hurt,* a first book of poems by E. J. Miller-Laino: "*Girl Hurt* records a woman's journey from the underworld of shame and hurt, where Mother cries 'like Frankenstein in the movie, / those deep, guttural half-words . . . / of monsters created with human hearts,' to the light of a recovered spirit. Miller-Laino's voice is vibrant and compelling in these intimate poems about family, work, and the hard road from silence into language." (Alice James)

James Welch recommends *Philadelphia Flowers,* poems by Roberta Hill Whiteman: "Once in a great while, a poet, like an eagle, catches a draft and soars to new heights. *Philadelphia Flowers* is that draft, and Roberta Hill Whiteman is that poet. This is an important, beautifully crafted book of poems by one of America's brightest poets." (Holy Cow)

EDITORS' CORNER

*New Books by
Our Advisory Editors*

James Carroll: *An American Requiem.* A stirring, generational memoir about Carroll's many lives as the son of an Air Force general, a priest, civil rights and antiwar activist, novelist, husband, and father. (Houghton Mifflin)

Donald Hall: *The Old Life.* An autobiography in verse by the venerable, witty, and always edifying poet and essayist. (Houghton Mifflin)

Robert Pinsky: *The Figured Wheel: New and Collected Poems 1966–1996.* This graceful, welcome collection gathers four of Pinsky's books, as well as new works. (Farrar, Straus & Giroux)

Christopher Tilghman: *Mason's Retreat.* Tilghman's arresting, much-anticipated first novel traces several generations of a family from its roots in England to a farm in Chesapeake Bay. (Random House)

CONTRIBUTOR SPOTLIGHT Born in 1941, Toi Derricotte grew up in Detroit, and when she thinks of her childhood, she remembers fear. "I had a need to be with people, but I was afraid of doing something wrong or saying the wrong thing." Her parents were getting divorced, a beloved grandmother had died, and Derricotte, an only child, was shunted into silence. As part of a middle-class, African-American family in the 1950's, she felt enormous familial pressure to conform, to disprove stereotypes—a repudiation of race and culture that came with a cost. In a poem called "Blackbottom" from her most recent book, *Captivity,* Derricotte writes about driving through a ghetto with her family: "Freshly escaped, black middle class, / we snickered, and were proud; / / We laughed at the bright clothes of a prostitute, / a man sitting on a curb with a bottle in his hand. / We smelled barbecue cooking in dented washtubs, and our mouths watered. / As much as we wanted it we couldn't take the chance."

From the time Derricotte was ten years old, writing poems became a source of both refuge and empowerment for her, giving voice to an emotional life that could not be shared or consoled. Only once did she dare to show her poems to a family member. When she was fourteen, her cousin, Melvin, was in medical school. He was taking an embryology class, and he allowed Derricotte to accompany him to the Chicago Museum, where they had fetuses and embryos on display. It was the first time anyone in her family had ever talked to Derricotte about conception, reproduction—*sex*—and she thought he might be receptive to her poems. Instead, after reading them, he said, "These are sick. Morbid." She didn't show her work to another soul again until she was twenty-seven.

At Wayne State University, psychology became her dominant academic interest, and she planned to pursue a Ph.D. in it, but her studies were interrupted when, at twenty, she had a child. She had to get out fast and make money. She switched her major to special education and, upon graduation, worked as a teacher. Eventually, she moved to Manhattan, ventured into writing workshops, and then obtained her master's degree in English and creative writing from NYU at the age of forty-three.

Since then, Derricotte's literary career has blossomed. She has published three collections of poetry: *The Empress of the Death House* (Lotus Press), *Natural Birth* (Crossing Press), and *Captivity* (Univ. of Pittsburgh Press). She has been the recipient of two fellowships from the NEA, as well as the Distinguished Pioneering of the Arts Award from the United Black Artists, the Lucille Medwick Memorial Award from the Poetry Society of America, and the Folger Shakespeare Library Poetry Book Award. Her poems have appeared in such magazines as *The American Poetry Review, Callaloo, The Paris Review,* and *The Kenyon Review,* and in numerous anthologies, including *The Pittsburgh Book of Contemporary American Poetry, A New Geography of Poets,* and *New American Poets of the '90s.* She has taught in the graduate creative writing programs at NYU, George Mason, and Old Dominion, and is now an associate professor of English at the University of Pittsburgh.

BRUCE DERRICOTTE

Each of Derricotte's autobiographical collections has represented a complex process of examination and reconciliation: "Every book for me is about reclaiming something that had been extinguished, reclaiming emotions, memories, parts of the self." With *The Empress of the Death House,* it was about "anger and sex." With *Natural Birth,* which focuses on giving birth to her son in a home for unwed mothers—a fact she didn't reveal to him until he was seventeen—it was about "shame." With *Captivity,* it was about "family, class, and race—a lot of scary poems."

"I feel the need to represent what's not spoken," she says. "I discover a pocket in myself that hasn't been articulated, then I have to find a form to carry that. Speaking the unspeakable is not that hard. The difficulty is in finding a way to make it perfect, to make it have light and beauty and truth inside it."

Clearly not shy of difficult subjects—race and gender, family and society—she embraces the contradictions that inevitably arise when approaching them. "I'm constantly trying to acknowledge the complications, rather than to simplify." About being light-skinned, for instance, she offers a long, elliptical, but provocative homily about race, identity, perception, and reality: "When I was a kid, the worst accusation that a black person could hurl at another black person was 'She think she white,' which meant 'She's not thinking right, she's crazy.' It's hitting at the very center of what one builds an ego on, a self. If you don't know what you are, how can you be a self? It's an insult that destroys the self in formation. What is 'light,' anyway? I had a dinner party for my mother not too long ago, and afterward, talking with my black friends about my relationship with her, they said that she is darker than I am, that I look more white. I had always thought that she was lighter than I am. Another time, after a reading, a black woman said to me, 'What makes you think you look white?' What makes people see what they think they see? And even further, how do we know that what they report they see is what they really see—even about themselves? Racism does funny things to mirrors. If reality is so twisted, how do we know what we see?

"I'm thinking of a story that this one woman, Carla Gary, told me. She had just moved into an all-white neighborhood, she's playing in the playground, she's five years old, and suddenly this white girl starts screaming, 'The nigger's going to get me, the nigger's going to get me,' and the girl starts running out of the playground. Carla runs after her, because *she's* scared, too. *Who's the nigger?* She's terrified. The white girl looks over her shoulder and sees her, and she screams even more because Carla is chasing after her. So Carla runs all the way home and she tells her mother, 'The nigger's going to get me, the nigger's going to get me,' and her mother is crying and laughing at the same time. She says, 'Carla, you *are* the nigger,' and Carla says, 'No, I'm not. I can't be. I can't be that thing that girl is screaming about.' "

Derricotte continues: "It's almost as if in order to accept that you're that terrible thing, you'd have to be crazy. In some ways, we're constantly running away from that terrifying self that we can't conceive as being us. There are so many things that can warp our sense of what's real. People would like to believe that you can look at someone and tell what they are. Because that would make you feel safe. Most poets know that's not the case."

At the moment, Derricotte is finishing a literary memoir, *The Black Notebooks,* which collects journal entries written over the past twenty years, and is at work on a new collection of poems. With Cornelius Eady, she is also preparing to run Cave Canem, a workshop retreat for African-American poets (with no tuition requirements) this summer in New York State.

In her mid-fifties now, Derricotte does not fight her designation as a black activist and feminist poet—labels that, ironically, sometimes introduce unfair limits—but she is hardly rigid, nor is she given to demagoguery. Rather, Derricotte is gregarious, unaffected, and youthful, and possesses an abundant sense of humor, even with the most serious of issues: "People would like inspiring books that tell them what to do, something like *Five Steps Not to Be a Racist,*" she says, laughing raucously. But then, as always, she becomes sincere about the matter at hand: "That's just not the truth. The easy solutions don't really prepare one for the hard work that needs to be done."

PHONE-A-POEM Phone-a-Poem is running again, thanks to Emerson College's Division of Writing, Literature, and Publishing. Overseen by the division's M.F.A. students, the service will present a different poet reading his or her work every two weeks (the tape will be changed on the first and fifteenth of each month). The new number is: (617) 824-8754.

FOUNDATION AWARDS Several *Ploughshares* writers have recently received foundation grants: Lucy Grealy, author of *Autobiography of a Face* and *Everyday Alibis,* and Mary Ruefle, author of the forthcoming *Cold Pluto,* were honored with $30,000 Whiting Writers' Awards. Rafael Campo, author of *The Other Man Was Me* and *The Poetry of Healing,* and George Packer, author of *The Village of Waiting* and *The Half Man,* were given $20,000 fellowships for literary nonfiction by the Echoing Green Foundation.

CONTRIBUTORS' NOTES

Spring 1996

ELIZABETH ALEXANDER is the author of *The Venus Hottentot* and has completed a second collection of poems, *Body of Life.* Her verse play, *Diva Studies,* will premiere at the Yale School of Drama in May 1996, and she is at work on a collection of essays, *On Black Masculinity.* She is currently teaching at Yale University while on leave from the University of Chicago.

JULIA ALVAREZ is the author of two novels, *How the García Girls Lost Their Accents* and *In the Time of the Butterflies,* and two books of poems, *Homecoming* and *The Other Side.* She teaches literature and creative writing at Middlebury College and is at work on a new novel.

RANE ARROYO is a gay Puerto Rican poet and playwright. His latest collection, *The Singing Shark,* is forthcoming from Bilingual Press this summer. *The House with Black Windows,* co-written with the poet Glenn Sheldon, was produced in 1995 by Polaris Theater in New York City. His papers are archived at El Centro de Estudios Puertorriqueños/Hunter College.

ALISON BRACKENBURY was born in England in 1953. Her work has won an Eric Gregory Award and a Poetry Book Society Recommendation. She has published five collections of poetry, most recently *1829* (Carcanet, 1995).

RAFAEL CAMPO teaches and practices medicine at Harvard Medical School's Beth Israel Hospital. *What the Body Told,* his second collection of poems, will be published by Duke University Press in April 1996; *The Poetry of Healing,* a collection of his prose, is due from W.W. Norton in September 1996. He recently received a fellowship for literary nonfiction from the Echoing Green Foundation.

MELISSA CANNON's work has recently appeared in *Bogg, The Kenyon Review,* and *The Lyric.* Her chapbook of poems, *Sister Fly Goes to Market,* was published by Truedog Press in 1980. She lives in Nashville, Tennessee, where she works in the fast food industry.

ALFRED CORN is the author of seven books of poetry. He teaches in the writing division of the School of the Arts at Columbia. "Musical Sacrifice" was completed after a visit to Leipzig and Prague last spring.

BRIAN KOMEI DEMPSTER completed his M.F.A. in creative writing at the University of Michigan, where he received the Academy of American Poets Award, a Cowden Fellowship, and the Hopwood Award. He also received a scholarship to attend the 1995 Bread Loaf Writers' Conference. His work recently appeared in *Quarterly West.*

TORY DENT's first collection of poems, *What Silence Equals,* was published by Persea Books in 1993. Her work has appeared in *The Paris Review, The Partisan Review, The Kenyon Review, Agni,* and other magazines, as well as in the anthologies *Life Sentences, The Exact Change Yearbook, In the Company of My Solitude,* and *Things Shaped in Passing.* She also writes arts criticism for magazines, including *Arts, Flash Art,* and *Parachute.*

TOI DERRICOTTE has published three collections of poetry: *Natural Birth* (Crossing), *The Empress of the Death House* (Lotus), and, most recently, *Captivity* (Univ. of Pittsburgh), which is in its fourth printing. *The Black Notebooks* will be published by W.W. Norton in 1997. She is a recipient of two fellowships from the NEA and the Distinguished Pioneering in the Arts Award from the United Black Artists, USA, Inc. She teaches in the creative writing program at the University of Pittsburgh.

CORNELIUS EADY is the author of five books of poetry, including *Victims of the Latest Dance Craze,* which was the Academy of American Poets' 1985 Lamont Poetry Selection, and *The Gathering of My Name,* which was nominated for the 1992 Pulitzer Prize in Poetry. He has received fellowships from the NEA, the Guggenheim Foundation, the Lila Wallace–Reader's Digest Fund, and the Rockefeller Foundation. He has taught poetry at Sarah Lawrence College, New York University, William and Mary, and is currently an associate professor of English and the director of the Poetry Center at SUNY Stony Brook.

THOMAS SAYERS ELLIS, a co-founding member of The Dark Room Collective, earned his M.F.A. from Brown University, and is currently a fellow at the Fine Arts Work Center in Provincetown, Massachusetts. Most recently his poems have appeared in *Between God and Gangsta Rap: Bearing Witness to Black Culture* and *The Garden Thrives: Twentieth-Century African-American Poetry.* In 1993, he co-edited *On the Verge: Emerging Poets and Artists,* and in March, his manuscript of poems, *The Good Junk,* was published in the first volume of the annual series *Take Three* from Graywolf Press.

MARTÍN ESPADA is the author of five poetry collections, most recently *City of Coughing and Dead Radiators* and *Imagine the Angels of Bread,* both from W.W. Norton. His awards include two NEA fellowships, the PEN/Revson Fellowship, and the Paterson Poetry Prize. Espada teaches in the English department at the University of Massachusetts–Amherst.

U. A. FANTHORPE, who was born in Kent and educated at Oxford, has worked as a teacher and a hospital reception clerk. The recipient of many prizes, she has published six collections of poems. She was a candidate for the position as the Oxford Professor of Poetry in the last election.

JULIE FAY's "Hannah" is a chapter from her recently completed novel *In the Houses of the Good People,* which is currently seeking a publisher. Her poetry collection, *Portraits of Women,* was published by Ahsahta Press in 1991. She lives in Blount's Creek, North Carolina, and Montpeyroux, France.

ANNE FINGER has published three books: a novel, *Bone Truth* (Coffee House, 1994), an autobiographical essay, *Past Due: A Story of Disability, Pregnancy and Birth* (Seal, 1990), and a short story collection, *Basic Skills* (Univ. of Missouri, 1988). Currently at work on a novel, she teaches creative writing at Wayne State University in Detroit, where she lives with her ten-year-old son, Max.

CATHERINE GAMMON is the author of the novel *Isabel Out of the Rain* (Mercury House, 1991). She has published stories most recently in *The Kenyon Review, Manoa,* and *Central Park.* She teaches in the M.F.A. program at the University of Pittsburgh.

DIANA GARCÍA, a native of California's San Joaquin Valley, recently moved from San Diego to Connecticut, where she is an assistant professor of English at Central Connecticut State University. Her work has appeared in *The Kenyon Review, Bloomsbury Review,* and *The Mid-American Review.*

MARY GORDON is the bestselling author of the novels *Final Payments, The Company of Women, Men and Angels,* and *The Other Side,* as well as a collection of stories, *Temporary Shelter,* and of essays, *Good Boys and Dead Girls.* She has received the Lila Acheson Wallace–Reader's Digest Writer's Award and a Guggenheim Fellowhip. She teaches at Barnard College. *Shadow Man,* a book about her father, will be published in May.

ARTHUR GREGOR's most recent collection, *The River Serpent and Other Poems,* was published by Sheep Meadow Press. Earlier volumes include *Selected Poems, The Past Now,* and others from Doubleday. He is also the author of a memoir, *A Longing in the Land,* published by Schocken Books.

JUDITH HALL's first book, *To Put the Mouth To,* was selected for the National Poetry Series and published by William Morrow. She serves as the poetry editor of *The Antioch Review.*

MARIE-GENEVIÈVE HAVEL is a Paris-based painter, engraver, and graphic artist. Since 1988, she has also created images with a computer-generated palette, one of which, *Tous les départs sont possibles,* appears on the cover. In April 1996, an exhibition of her prints and computer graphics will be on view at the Alliance Française in Cork, Ireland; a one-woman show of her work in all media was exhibited at the Maison de l'Avocat in Nantes in December 1995. Her work has been shown all over France, as well as in Belgium, Morocco, Brazil, and Argentina.

JOHN R. KEENE is the author of *Annotations* (New Directions, 1995), which was named one of *Publishers Weekly's* "Best Books of 1995" and earned a Critics' Choice 1995–1996 Award from the *San Francisco Review of Books* and *Today's First Edition.* He is a *New York Times* Fellow at New York University.

YUSEF KOMUNYAKAA's latest book, *Neon Vernacular,* published by Wesleyan University Press, was awarded the 1994 Pulitzer Prize and the Kingsley Tufts Award. He also received the 1994 William Faulkner Prize (Université de Rennes). He teaches creative writing and literature at Indiana University.

MAXINE KUMIN's eleventh book of poems, *Connecting the Dots,* will be published by W.W. Norton in July. Her book of essays and stories, *Women, Animals, and Vegetables,* focusing for the most part on women, is now out in paperback from Ontario Review Press. She is a newly elected chancellor of the Academy of American Poets and the 1995 winner of the Aiken Taylor Poetry Prize. Kumin and her husband live on a farm in New Hampshire, where they raise horses.

ADRIAN C. LOUIS teaches on the Pine Ridge Reservation of South Dakota and is a recent recipient of the Lila Wallace–Reader's Digest Writer's Award. His new collection of short stories, *Wild Indians & Other Creatures,* is now available from the University of Nevada Press.

KHALED MATTAWA is the author of *Isamailia Eclipse* (Sheep Meadow, 1995). His poems have appeared in *Poetry, The Kenyon Review, New England Review, Callaloo, Crazyhorse, Poetry East, Michigan Quarterly Review, The Iowa Review, Black Warrior Review,* and *The Pushcart Prize XIX* (1994–1995). He was awarded the Alfred Hodder Fellowship at Princeton University for 1995–96.

STEPHEN MCLEOD's poems have appeared in *Agni, The American Poetry Review, Poetry East, Shenandoah,* and elsewhere. New work is forthcoming in *The Journal, The Paris Review, The Southwest Review,* and *Western Humanities Review.* He lives in New York City, where he is studying law at Fordham University.

CONSTANCE MERRITT is a doctoral candidate at the University of Nebraska–Lincoln, where, in 1994, she was awarded the Academy of American Poets College Prize for "Woman of Color."

ALICIA OSTRIKER is a poet and critic whose most recent book, *The Nakedness of the Fathers: Biblical Visions and Revisions,* combines prose and poetry. A new volume of poems, *The Crack in Everything,* is forthcoming this spring from the University of Pittsburgh Press.

CARL PHILLIPS is the author of two collections, *Cortège* (Graywolf, 1995) and *In the Blood* (Northeastern Univ., 1992). On leave this year from Washington University in St. Louis, where he teaches creative writing, English, and African-American literature, he is Visiting Assistant Professor in English and American Literature and Language at Harvard University.

MINNIE BRUCE PRATT's second book of poetry, *Crime Against Nature,* was nominated for a Pulitzer Prize, chosen as the 1989 Lamont Poetry Selection by the Academy of American Poets, and received the American Library Association's Gay and Lesbian Book Award for Literature. Her other books include *We Say We Love Each Other, Rebellion: Essays 1980–1991,* and *S/HE,* stories about gender boundary crossing. She is presently working on a series of narrative poems, *Walking Back Up Depot Street.* She lives in Jersey City, New Jersey.

HILDA RAZ is the author of two poetry collections, *What is Good* (Thorn Tree) and *The Bone Dish* (State Street). Her poems, essays, and reviews have appeared or are forthcoming in *Touchstones: American Poets on a Favorite Poem, American Nature Writers, The Whole Story: Editors on Fiction, The Southern Review, Women's Review of Books, The Laurel Review,* and elsewhere. She is Associate Professor of English at the University of Nebraska–Lincoln, where she edits *Prairie Schooner.*

BOYER RICKEL is Assistant Director of the creative writing program at the University of Arizona. His book of poems, *arreboles,* was published by Wesleyan/University Press of New England.

ALEIDA RODRÍGUEZ's poetry has been published in *The Progressive, Prairie Schooner,* and *The Kenyon Review,* and her prose is forthcoming in *In Short* (Norton, 1996). *Garden of Exile* was a finalist for the National Poetry Series and runner-up for the Barnard New Women Poets Prize. In 1995, she was also a finalist for the Pablo Neruda Prize.

CAROL RUMENS is the author most recently of *Best China Sky* and *Thinking of Skins: New & Selected Poems,* both from Bloodaxe Books. She lives in Northern Ireland.

GRACE SCHULMAN's latest poetry collection is *For That Day Only* (Sheep Meadow, 1995). Her previous books of poetry include *Hemispheres* and *Burn Down the Icons.* Her work appears in *The Best American Poetry 1995,* and she is a 1995 Fellow in Poetry of the New York Foundation of the Arts. She is Poetry Editor of *The Nation* and a professor of English at Baruch College, CUNY.

MAUREEN SEATON is the author of three books of poetry, most recently *Furious Cooking,* which won the Iowa Prize for Poetry and is forthcoming this spring from the University of Iowa Press. In 1994, she was the recipient of grants from the Illinois Arts Council and the NEA. Her poems have appeared in *The Atlantic, The Paris Review, The New Republic, Ploughshares,* and *The Pushcart Prize XX.*

REGINALD SHEPHERD's first book of poems, *Some Are Drowning* (Univ. of Pittsburgh), won the 1993 AWP Award; his second, *Angel, Interrupted,* is due from Pittsburgh this fall. He is the recipient of a 1995 NEA Fellowship, among other awards, and has been selected for the 1995 and 1996 editions of *The Best American Poetry.*

EDMUND WHITE's "The Tea Ceremony" is from his novel *The Farewell Symphony,* which is scheduled for publication in 1997. The novel will complete the trilogy begun with *A Boy's Own Story* and *The Beautiful Room Is Empty.* White's biography of Jean Genet won the National Book Critics Circle Award.

～

SUBSCRIBERS Please note that on occasion we exchange mailing lists with other literary magazines and organizations. If you would like your name excluded from these exchanges, simply send us a letter stating so. Also, please inform us when you move. The post office usually will not forward journals.

SUBMISSION POLICIES *Ploughshares* is published three times a year: usually mixed issues of poetry and fiction in the Winter and Spring and a fiction issue in the Fall, with each guest-edited by a different writer. We welcome unsolicited manuscripts from August 1 to March 31 (postmark dates). All submissions sent from April to July are returned unread. In the past, guest editors often announced specific themes for issues, but we have revised our editorial policies and no longer restrict submissions to thematic topics. Submit your work at any time during our reading period; if a manuscript is not timely for one issue, it will be considered for another. Send one prose piece and/or one to three poems at a time (mail genres separately). Poems should be individually typed either single- or double-spaced on one side of the page. Prose should be typed double-spaced on one side and be no longer than twenty-five pages. Although we look primarily for short stories, we occasionally publish personal essays/memoirs. Novel excerpts are acceptable if self-contained. Unsolicited book reviews and criticism are not considered. Please do not send multiple submissions of the same genre, and do not send another manuscript until you hear about the first. Additional submissions will be returned unread. Mail your manuscript in a page-sized manila envelope, your full name and address written on the outside, to the "Fiction Editor," "Poetry Editor," or "Nonfiction Editor." (Unsolicited work sent directly to a guest editor's home or office will be discarded.) All manuscripts and correspondence regarding submissions should be accompanied by a self-addressed, stamped envelope (S.A.S.E.) for a response. Expect three to five months for a decision. Do not query us until five months have passed, and if you do, please write to us, including an S.A.S.E. and indicating the postmark date of submission, instead of calling. Simultaneous submissions are amenable as long as they are indicated as such and we are notified immediately upon acceptance elsewhere. We cannot accommodate revisions, changes of return address, or forgotten S.A.S.E.'s after the fact. We do not reprint previously published work. Translations are welcome if permission has been granted. We cannot be responsible for delay, loss, or damage. Payment is upon publication: $25/printed page, $50 minimum per title, $250 maximum per author, with two copies of the issue and a one-year subscription.

THE NAME *Ploughshares* 1. The sharp edge of a plough that cuts a furrow in the earth. 2a. A variation of the name of the pub, the Plough and Stars, in Cambridge, Massachusetts, where a journal was founded. 2b. The pub's name was inspired by the Sean O'Casey play about the Easter Rising of the Irish "citizen army." The army's flag contained a plough, representing the things of the earth, hence practicality; and stars, the ideals by which the plough is steered. 3. A shared, collaborative, community effort that has endured for twenty-five years. 4. A literary journal that has been energized by a desire for harmony, peace, and reform. Once, that spirit motivated civil rights marches, war protests, and student activism. Today, it still inspirits a desire for beating swords into ploughshares, but through the power and the beauty of the written word.

American Short Fiction

JOSEPH E. KRUPPA, Editor

INCLUDING SUCH AUTHORS AS:

Reynolds Price • Joyce Carol Oates
David Michael Kaplan
Naguib Mahfouz • Ursula K. Le Guin
Theodore Weesner
Lynne Sharon Schwartz
Debra Jo Immergut

National Magazine Award for Fiction
1993 and 1995 Finalist

American Short Fiction is published in
Spring (March), Summer (June), Fall (September), and
Winter (December)

Subscriptions: Individual $24, Institution $36
Outside USA, add $6/Subscription

Single Copy Rates:
Individual $9.95, Institution $12, Outside USA, add $2/copy
Prepayment only, please.
Refunds available only on unshipped quantities of current subscriptions.

To subscribe, or for more information, write:
University of Texas Press
Journals Division
Box 7819, Austin, Texas 78713–7819
journals@uts.cc.utexas.edu

Ploughshares Patrons

This publication would not be possible without the support of
our readers and the generosity of the following individuals
and organizations. As a nonprofit enterprise,
we welcome donations of any amount.

COUNCIL: $3,000 for two lifetime subscriptions, acknowledgement
in the journal for three years, and votes on the Cohen and Zacharis
Awards. PATRON: $1,000 for a lifetime subscription and acknow-
ledgement in the journal for two years. FRIEND: $500 for a life-
time subscription and acknowledgement in the journal
for one year. All donations are tax-deductible.
Please make your check payable to *Ploughshares*,
Emerson College, 100 Beacon St., Boston, MA 02116.

Take Three

AGNI *New Poets Series: 1*

Published by Graywolf Press, edited by the poetry panel of *AGNI* magazine, *Take Three* is the first in an important series designed to launch the work of young poets.

Take **Thomas Sayers Ellis:** At the center of Ellis's work is the figure of an aggressive father, taunting his son into song. Ellis's fractured syntax, the spasmodic, staccato utterance suggest a defiant sensibility. Yet it's the sweet exuberance, the delight in kinship, that makes these poems *fly.*

Take **Joe Osterhaus:** "Osterhaus's poems dramatize his struggle to gather back from the world an objective sense of what Keats once called 'the principle of beauty in all things.' Passionate, musical, intelligent, this is work of great integrity and powerfully rendered feeling." TOM SLEIGH

Take **Larissa Szporluk:** "If those two strange, haunted beings, Emily Dickinson and Georg Trakl, wedded, these poems might well be the offspring. Faced with such rending beauty, such ravished lucidity, all we can do is stand back and gaze with gratitude and awe." GREGORY ORR

PAPERBACK, $12.95, 1-55597-239-X

GRAYWOLF PRESS
2402 University Avenue · Suite 203
Saint Paul · Minnesota 55114
612-641-0077 · FAX 612-641-0036

MFA in Writing
at Vermont College

Intensive 11-Day Residencies
July and January on the beautiful Vermont
campus, catered by the
New England Culinary Institute.
Workshops, classes, readings,
conferences, followed by

Non-Resident 6-Month Writing Projects
in poetry and fiction individually designed
during residency.
In-depth criticism of manuscripts.
Sustained dialogue with faculty.

Post-Graduate Writing Semester
for those who have already finished
a Graduate degree
with a concentration in creative writing.

For More Information
Roger Weingarten
MFA Writing Program, Box 889
Vermont College of Norwich University
Montpelier, VT 05602
802–828–8840

Vermont College admits students regardless of race,
creed, sex or ethnic origin.

Scholarships, minority scholarships and
financial aid available.

Low-residency B.A. & M.A. programs
also available.

POETRY FACULTY
Robin Behn
Mark Cox
Deborah Digges
Nancy Eimers
Mark Halliday
Richard Jackson
Sydney Lea
Jack Myers
William Olsen
David Rivard
J. Allyn Rosser
Mary Ruefle
Betsy Sholl
Leslie Ullman
Roger Weingarten
David Wojahn

FICTION FACULTY
Carol Anshaw
Tony Ardizzone
Phyllis Barber
Francois Camoin
Abby Frucht
Douglas Glover
Diane Lefer
Ellen Lesser
Bret Lott
Sena Jeter Naslund
Christopher Noel
Pamela Painter
Sharon Sheehe Stark
Gladys Swan
W.D. Wetherell

Be an Expatriate Writer for Two Weeks.

Join an international group of selected fiction writers for an intensive working seminar in the tranquillity of a Dutch Renaissance castle. Guided by six distinguished instructors, this seminar is designed to be intimate and productive. The team taught workshop is an editorial roundtable where writers are advised on strategies for analyzing structure and developing and sustaining character-in-action. Designated writing sessions and individual conferences enable new or revised work and redefined writing objectives. The seminar concentrates on the craft and technique of fiction while also considering the pragmatics of the literary market. The dynamics of the seminar are carefully planned to include both published writers and those in the early stages of promising careers. The seminar is sponsored by Emerson College and inspired by the literary traditions of the journal *Ploughshares*, an Emerson College publication. Four academic credits are offered and all applications received by April 1 are considered for a $500 fellowship. DIRECTOR: Alexandra Marshall. FACULTY: James Carroll, Pamela Painter, Thomas E. Kennedy, Alexandra Johnson, Askold Melnyczuk. WRITER-IN-RESIDENCE: Robie Macauley. VISITING WRITER: John Updike.

Seventh Annual

Ploughshares International Fiction Writing Seminar

Kasteel Well
The Netherlands
August 20-31, 1996
Emerson College
European Center

BENNINGTON
SUMMER
WRITING
WORKSHOPS

June 30-July 13 &
July 14-27,
1996

■

2-week or 4-week residencies in

Fiction, Nonfiction, Poetry

ACADEMIC CREDIT
AVAILABLE

For more information, contact:
Priscilla Hodgkins, Assistant Director
Bennington Summer Writing Workshops
Bennington College, Box S
Bennington, Vermont 05201
802-442-5401, ext. 160
Fax: 802-442-6164

wc&f

FACULTY:

Elizabeth Cox	Marcie Hershman
C. Michael Curtis	Jonathan Holden
Thomas Disch	Ann Hood
Lynn Emanuel	Rick Moody
George Garrett	Ed Ochester
David Gates	Bruce Weigl
Lucy Grealy	Meg Wolitzer

READERS:

Russell Banks	Rebecca Godwin
Richard Bausch	Matthew Graham
Frank Bidart	Donald Hall
David Broza	Liam Rector
Wyn Cooper	Chase Twichell

PLUS PUBLISHERS & LITERARY FOLK:

James Atlas
New York Times Magazine

David Fenza
Associated Writing Programs

Sarah Gorham
Sarabande Books

Don Lee
Ploughshares

Fiona McCrae
Graywolf Press

Jeanne McCulloch
Paris Review

Ed Morrow
Northshire Bookstore

Carol Houck Smith
W.W. Norton & Co

Geri Thoma
Elaine Markson (Literary) Agency

Pat Towers
Elle Magazine

William Wadsworth
Academy of American Poets

Bruce Wilcox
University of Massachusetts Press

Fine Arts Work Center in Provincetown

SUMMER WORKSHOPS & RESIDENCIES 1996
one-week workshops • June 23–August 31

Fiction

Dean Albarelli	Pam Houston	Rick Moody
Anne Bernays	Tama Janowitz	Ann Patchett
Michael Cunningham	Fred Leebron	Susan Power
Peter Ho Davies	Carole Maso	Heidi Jon Schmidt
Maria Flook	Richard McCann	A.J. Verdelle

Poetry

Mark Doty	Cleopatra Mathis	Liz Rosenberg
Marie Howe	Gail Mazur	Tom Sleigh
Yusef Komunyakaa	Susan Mitchell	Charlie Smith
	Robert Pinsky	

Memoir & Biography

Hope Edelman	Justin Kaplan	Michael Ryan
Lucy Grealy	Susanna Kaysen	

Screenwriting & Genre

Pat Cooper	Nelson Gidding	Bill Phillips
	Jackie Manthorne	

for catalog or more information, contact:

Peter Ho Davies, Summer Program Coordinator
Fine Arts Work Center, 24 Pearl Street, Provincetown, MA 02657
Tel: 508-487-9960 • Fax: 508-487-8873

BENNINGTON WRITING SEMINARS

MFA in Writing and Literature
Two-year low-residency program

FICTION
NONFICTION
POETRY

For more information contact:
Writing Seminars,
Box PL, Bennington College
Bennington, Vermont 05201
802-442-5401, ext. 160

The Madison Review

A literary magazine published semiannually by the University of Wisconsin
Department of English

announces its

PHYLLIS SMART YOUNG POETRY PRIZE
&
CHRIS O'MALLEY FICTION PRIZE

WINNERS OF THE YOUNG AND O'MALLEY PRIZES
RECIEVE $500 AND PUBLICATION IN THE MADISON REVIEW.
ALL ENTRIES MUST BE RECEIVED IN THE MONTH OF SEPTEMBER.
SEND ONE STORY OR THREE POEMS
(POEMS SHOULD BE UNDER FOUR PAGES EACH).
MANUSCRIPTS WILL NOT BE RETURNED.
ENTRY FEE IS $3.00 PAYABLE TO THE MADISON REVIEW.
INCLUDE SASE WITH ALL CORRESPONDENCES AND SUBMISSIONS.

YOUNG/O'MALLEY PRIZES
c/o THE MADISON REVIEW
UNIVERSITY OF WISCONSIN-MADISON
DEPARTMENT OF ENGLISH
MADISON, WI   53706

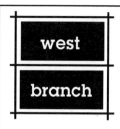